Lessons from a Bird

And Other Life Reflections

Janette McGowen

Copyright © 2014 Janette McGowen

All rights reserved.

ISBN-13: 978-1500524661
ISBN-10: 1500524662

DEDICATION

To my parents, J.B. & Nellie Ruth McGowan, who have loved and inspired my siblings and me for 57 years of marriage.
Love You, Mama & Daddy. ♥

****

A portion of the net proceeds from the sale of this book will be donated to the David Jones, Jr. Assisted Living Center in Nashville TN. It is a 501(c)(3) organization and a ministry of the Schrader Lane Church of Christ.

CONTENTS

Acknowledgements

Introduction

Reflections

About Author

Lessons from a Bird

Chapter 1 Lessons from a Bird..15

Chapter 2 If You Want a Man to be a Man…Let Him!! 16

Chapter 3 When Life is "Raining Down"...............................18

Chapter 4 "…Make It Real or else Forget About It…" 20

Chapter 5 "Lean Not On Your Own Understanding…" 21

Chapter 6 "You Have The Right To Remain Silent…" 23

Chapter 7 "GET OVER IT!" – The worst advice… 25

Chapter 8 "The Way We Were…" 28

Chapter 9 Searching for Ranch Dressing 30

Chapter 10 "Living a Long Life or a Life Well-Lived…" 34

Chapter 11 The Prodigal Son's Brother 37

Chapter 12 "Thrill of Victory - Agony of Defeat" 42

Chapter 13 I Need You, My Friend… 44

Chapter 14 Heavenly-Minded or Earthly-Good? 46

Chapter 15 The Other Shoe 49

Chapter 16 FORGIVE While...Remembering??? 52

Chapter 17 Are You TOO BUSY??? 55

Chapter 18 Fading into Obscurity... 57

Chapter 19 "No Matter Where You Go, There You Are..." 60

Chapter 20 Answer to Our Prayers 62

Chapter 21 Seeing the Unseen in 2014 66

Chapter 22 Be "Good For Nothing" 68

Chapter 23 "Are Ya' Feeling Me???" 70

Chapter 24 "To Everything There is a Season..." 72

Chapter 25 Going Through Your Stuff... 74

Chapter 26 My "Way of Thinking" 76

Chapter 27 Not About Me… …………………………………78

Chapter 28 "Cut Off Your Nose to Spite Your Face…" ……..81

Chapter 29 Do You Really Want It? …………………………..83

Chapter 30 Down Off the Pedestal …………………………..85

Chapter 31 You Have Benn DISMISSED… ………………..88

Chapter 32 Rising to your Expectations ……………………..90

Chapter 33 Settling for Mediocrity ………………………..…..93

Chapter 34 Spectator of Our Own Lives……………………..95

Chapter 35 I Can't Want It More……………………………..97

Chapter 36 My Favorite "Insult" ……………………………..100

Chapter 37 Not Trying to Get Political…But… …………….103

Chapter 38 Judging vs. Good Judgment……………………..105

Chapter 39 Understanding the 23rd Psalm…………………...107

Chapter 40 "Are You Relevant in the 21st Century?"..............109

Chapter 41 "Ain't Nobody Got Time For That!"......................114

Chapter 42 Why We Do What We Do? 116

Chapter 43 Will God Even Recognize You? 118

Chapter 44 "What's in Your (Spiritual) Wallet?" 120

Chapter 45 Blessing or Lesson? 122

Chapter 46 Unsolicited Advice 124

Chapter 47 Trouble at the Gate....................................127

Chapter 48 "Thrown Under the Bus" 130

Chapter 49 "Float Like a Butterfly, Sting Like a Bee…" 132

Chapter 50 "Exercises" to Avoid and Embrace 134

Chapter 51 "Because I'm Happy!" 137

Chapter 52 "Get Busy Living or Get Busy Dying…" 140

Janette McGowen

Acknowledgements

I first and foremost, give all glory and honor to our Lord and Savior Jesus Christ, who is the center of my existence.

This book would not have been possible without many "prayer warriors" and "angels," simple messengers from the Lord, to begin this journey.

My humblest gratitude is to the Lord, who blessed me to be parented by such phenomenal human beings as J.B. and Nellie Ruth McGowan. They exerted pure love….sometimes tough, but always consistent… and never unwavering. I try to model myself by them every day and always want to make them proud of who I have become and continue to evolve into.

Many thanks for the tireless efforts of my publishing company, CreateSpace Publishing, who helped make this heart-inspired, personal project materialize. I couldn't have done it without you.

I must give thanks to two people who have and continue to be my mentors, confidants and dear friends: Dr. David Jones, Jr. and Constance W. Elliott. **Bro. Jones** has been the Minister of the Schrader Lane Church of Christ in Nashville, Tennessee for the past 52 years. You have given me inspiration, wisdom, reprimand when needed, encouragement and a belief in my abilities that often scares me. You have and will continue to be my source of guidance and unconditional affirmation. **Connie Elliott**…you took me under your wing when I was a scattered, feisty and hard-headed young woman…and stuck with me, for over 21 years now, loving me with all of my imperfection. Your quite elegance, gentle tenacity and youthful grace are hallmarks that I strive to shape my life toward every day.

I would not have been able to finally move this project forward without the firm yet compassionate "nudge" and guidance of David Jones III, Kenneth R. Anderson, Carlos Greene, and especially, **my** nephew, Jonathan McGowen, who often told me to ***"stop talking about it and be about it."***

There are others that have helped influence and inspire me along the way, especially with overwhelming encouragement of my writing ability and my blog.

Sincere gratitude to my sisters Billye Jean James, Annette Sanders and Yevette McGowen; my niece, Rikita Word; my brothers-in-law Robert James and Eddie Sanders; as well as Alberto Guzman, Ms. Jessie Waggoner, Anne Bailey, Joseph Edmonson, Charles P. Edmonson, Megan Evans-Carlotta, Renita Cobb, John & Bridget Lane, Joyce Dungee Proctor, Carolyne Jones, Lurried Vinson, Sr., Angela Grace, Wayne McGowan, Mona Faye Pryor, Rose Hollis, Antoinette Foy, Tanza Pride, Kirsten Jones, Kimbrea Browning, Robert Gardenhire, Timothy McCleskey, Sr., Chris Whitaker, Sr., Leonard "Duke" & Mary Wellington, Grady & Amy McNeal, Mr. Dion Allen, Sarah Henderson, Ruth Henderson, Vincent Taylor, Kim Sanford, Mary Wade and Jack Witherspoon. Humble thanks also to renowned author Amy Hill Hearth, whose gift of writing continues to inspire me.

There are many others…you know who you are….so does God.

Introduction

I have always loved to write. I still have a diary that I constructed with string and a cardboard box when I was age 6 and just learning to write.

I never made anything less than "A's" in English, Spelling or Writing from 1st Grade through College. I made all "A's" on papers written every week of 13, grueling, 6-week classes while working on my MBA. I was stunned when the instructors would often say, "This is excellent, Graduate Level Writing." Yet, it was a skill I continued to minimize and ignore.

However, about two years ago, I was halted in my tracks with a diagnosis of Primary Progressive Multiple Sclerosis. Are you kidding me? I had always "prided" myself in being a Health Fanatic. How could this have slipped in? My emotions ran the gamut – from denial – to "just fix it" – to mild depression.

During this time, my job was eliminated. Going through the tedious process of "redefining" my life left me a lot of time alone…mostly, in silence.

I found solace in being on my computer via Social Media and journaling.

I tend to suffer from "paralysis by analysis." A few friends in the past had recommended I consider blogging. They noted that I always appear to have thought-provoking comments on Facebook.

One day, January 13, 2014 to be exact, I was analyzing the more popular blogging sites, WordPress and Google's Blogger, to see which one I liked most. I went back and forth for hours. While back at Blogger, I saw a button that said CREATE BLOG. I thought I may see what creating a blog entailed, back out of it and then continue my analysis of the two.

When I clicked it…it said "Blog Successfully Created." NO!!! I wasn't trying to do that!! As I panicked and tried to figure out how to delete it, my "inner voice" whispered, "We are already in. Let's give it a try, shall we?" And it has been like a thrilling, roller-coaster ride ever since…

My blog has guided me toward writing this book. My reflections are truly inspired…by family, friends, church members, former work colleagues, acquaintances, strangers, life experiences, mistakes made, lessons learned, solemn regrets, epiphanies, observations…and most importantly, by my Heavenly Father.

Every day, I humbly pray, "Lord, I know I asked you to use me. Although I don't know what you are doing with me right now, for once in my life, I'm going to surrender to it and enjoy the journey – pot-holes, curves, gravel, dirt roads, wind, rain, hail, snow, lack of visibility, sunshine, cool breeze, rainbows…all of it…"

It is my prayer that these "life reflections" resonate with you and give you hope, insight, humor and comfort as we all navigate this bumpy, uncertain journey called LIFE.

1
Lessons from a Bird...

Back in July 2013, while hurriedly driving out of my driveway en route to a corporate appointment, a white bird flew down and stood squarely in my path.

Not wanting to hurt it, I hit my brakes, anticipating that it would fly away.

It stood still, stared at me, and didn't budge! (Are you kidding me???)

We just looked at each other. Time stood still.

It's body language appeared to say,

"Slow your roll, Human. I will move...*When I'm Ready*."

I didn't know whether to be frustrated or laugh! Shock? Awe? or LOL?

I chose to Laugh-Out-Loud...at this bird's apparent gall, arrogance and audacity!

It finally...slowly... strutted away.

<u>Lessons Learned</u>:
#1. Life doesn't have to be so rushed and hectic.
#2. Breathe.
#3. Patience.
#4. Respect nature and God's creatures.
#5. Find humor in the ordinary.

God teaches us big lessons in the smallest ways. Too funny!☺

2
If You Want a Man to be a Man…Let Him!

An older "gentleman"…dear friend, church member and mentor wanted to thank me for the card I had sent him, my simple gesture of remembering his birthday, by taking me to lunch.

He INSISTED on picking me up.
(I offered to just meet him).
He INSISTED on driving through a torrential rain storm to get me.
(I offered to cancel because of the rain. I wasn't that important…)
He INSISTED on opening my car door for me.
(I was preparing to get out on my own like I always do.)
He INSISTED on holding my umbrella for me to keep me from getting rained on.
He INSISTED on holding the door open for me.
He INSISTED on me sitting down first.
He INSISTED on paying the check.
He INSISTED on waiting for me while I went to the restroom.
He INSISTED on holding the door open for me as we exited the restaurant.
He INSISTED on holding the door open for me when I got back in his car.
He INSISTED on driving responsibly.
(You consider me precious cargo???)
He INSISTED on opening my car door for me.
He INSISTED on walking me to my door.

I had seen him do this with his wife of 46 years. I thought it was endearing, but not practical. I considered him "Old School." I wasn't accustomed to being "vulnerable" to anyone.

Why did I find this treatment unnecessary, "uncalled for" and somewhat uncomfortable?

Why, as women, are we now so conditioned to BE STRONG, BE INDEPENDENT, and BE IN CONTROL???

The Big Lesson here:

You say you want a MAN to honor and cherish you, and treat you like a Queen.

Well then...Y*ou've Got to Let Him*....

3
"Power of the Human Touch..."

I was reminded of this while attending a funeral.

I was in the restroom. While waiting on my aunt, I sat in the waiting area in a comfortable lounge chair.

Suddenly a very young mother came in looking frantically around with a young girl in her arms. I would estimate the baby's age to be about 10-months-old. She was dressed beautifully, in a silky, pink, taffeta dress, with hair bows to match. The mother appeared to be looking for a changing station.

Since I was a member of this church, I told her, "There is no official changing station in this restroom. You might want to change her on the make-up station in front of us." She quickly said, "Oh...Ok."

Before I could say anything further, she began taking off her coat. She then asked, "Could you hold her for me?"

I gasped! Since I do not have children, this is not something I do on a regular basis.

Before I could close my mouth...she abruptly plopped the baby girl into my lap! The baby looked at me, then back at her mother. Her reaction reminded me of a line from the movie, *The Color Purple*: "Harpo? Who dis woman?"

I recovered quickly, held the child securely, and looked into her innocent eyes. The depth of those young eyes were so authentic...so pure...they melted my heart. I felt as though she was staring at my soul...

The young mother, appearing to feel reassured her daughter was in safe hands, went about her task of preparing to change her daughter. I bounced the baby on my lap, and smiled at her. I said, "You are so pretty!" The baby smiled and continued to intensely watch me.

Within a few minutes, the young mother told me "Thank You," and took the child from my arms. The child continued to look at me over her mother's shoulder, as I left.

This simple interaction reminded me of how powerful our touch can be to someone.

"Too often we underestimate the power of a touch, a smile, a kind word, a listening ear, an honest compliment, or the smallest act of caring, all of which have the potential to turn a life around." - Leo Buscaglia

We should NEVER take something so profound, yet so simple, for granted...

4
"...Make It Real or else Forget About It..."

I was dressing for an elegant affair one evening. My sister's sorority was hosting their Annual Christmas Ball. I decided to "be brave" and attend.

I did what most women do. All day long, I tried on dress after dress. Which one would make me look thinner? Girdle or Spanx?

Finally...I sang to myself *Smooth* by Carlos Santana, featuring Rob Thomas..."Give me your heart, **Make It Real,** or else **FORGET ABOUT IT!**"

I'm just going to wear what I have...period.

I entered the ballroom...looking confident on the outside...major insecurity on the inside. I paused to look around. Women were there...all shapes, sizes and colors...just being themselves. The men with them looked proud to have them by their sides. I realized that they were not focusing on me. They were busy assessing their own selves.

I had to admire these women. They were going with what they had, confidently...focused on having an enjoyable evening.

I decided to adapt the same attitude. Interesting what a shift in attitude can give you.

"Change the way you look at things and the things you look at change." - Dr. Wayne Dyer.

I decided to tell my "inner critic" to SHUT UP and just have a great time.

And... guess what?

I did...

5
"Lean Not On Your Own Understanding…"

One of my favorite Bible scriptures is:
Proverbs 3:5-6 (NKJV):
5 Trust in the Lord with all your heart,
And lean not on your own understanding;
6 In all your ways acknowledge Him,
And He shall direct your paths.

As I mature, I now resolve that I cannot "Lean on my Own Understanding." I am now coming to grips with the fact that I am not meant to understand everything. That is why I am supposed to just TRUST HIM.

Cases in point:
I don't understand…why people can wear $2 million dollar "bling" around their necks or on their fingers; when, for only about $55,000 each, they could build 36 Habitat-for-Humanity Homes – an entire community?
I don't understand…why celebrities and athletes seem to believe they earned that Oscar, Grammy, Emmy, Tony, Golden Globe, Olympic Gold Medal, World Cup, Wimbledon Tennis, or NBA-NFL-MLB Championship Ring all by themselves…with no help from GOD?
I don't understand…why we now seem to honor and have more respect for animals than Human Beings?
I don't understand…why people demand that you agree with their point-of-view; and when you don't, accuse you of HATE?
I don't understand…why everyone wants a gun, yet school shootings and gun violence have increased?
I don't understand…why children get sick and die?
I don't understand…why we no longer seem to "respect our elders?"

I don't understand…why "marriage" has become such a joke, with divorce rates exceeding 50% ? What happened to "for better or worse, through sickness and in health, forsaking all others, for as long as we both shall live… ???"

I don't understand…why do we seem to think we created ourselves and know more about our lives than our CREATOR?

I don't understand…why Good People seem to DIE too soon?

I don't understand…why people are late to worship the LORD on Sunday morning, but on-time for their job on Monday morning?

Why…I Ask?
And the answer I must accept is…*It's Not Mine to Know…*

6
"You Have The Right To Remain Silent…"

We often think of this phrase as one stated by the Police, advising the suspect of his or her "Miranda Rights." This warning is read after an arrest has been made and before police questioning is conducted.

The Miranda Warning says:
"You have the right to remain silent. Anything you say can and will be used against you in a court of law. You have the right to an attorney. If you cannot afford an attorney, one will be provided for you. Do you understand the rights I have just read to you?"
 http://www.mirandarights.org/prearrestquestioning.html

This warning also has implications for everyday life.

Once in my past, I went through a very rough time. I know I must have been a juicy subject of gossip. One of the most profound pieces of advice I received was from my Daddy. A normally mild-mannered man, he fiercely and adamantly told me: *"You don't owe anyone an explanation of your life!"*

Another learning lesson happened several years ago. I experienced some unexpected health issues that temporarily affected my speech. It resulted in my stuttering. I found myself "not talking" in fear of a relapse. This was an eye-opening experience. It is amazing what you learn when you are forced to BE QUIET. You hear a lot of things you normally wouldn't because you have typically been doing all of the talking.

We ALL should be very thoughtful of our conversation. Your words reveal to others exactly who you are. I love Maya Angelou's quote: *"When people show you (tell you) who they are, believe them the first time."*

People can ask you anything they choose. You have the right and choice as to how you respond.

Sometimes, the best response is NO RESPONSE.

"Silence is only frightening to people who are compulsively verbalizing." - William S. Burroughs

Silence IS Golden.

Remember…**You Have the RIGHT to Remain Silent…**

Learn to exercise this right.

Shhh…

7
"GET OVER IT!" – The worst advice...

One of my personal "pet peeves" is hearing people give others the advice of: *"Get Over It!"*

I personally interpret that as to "ignore it" and "move on," as if it didn't happen.

I tried many times to do this, but it just didn't work for me. I still found myself "stuck" on what had happened to me or what someone had done to me years earlier. Yes...my outer actions appeared as though I had "gotten over it." However, my heart was still very heavy, and emotionally, I was a mess.

Someone even recently gave me this advice as a means to manage my new health issues and pull myself out of my mini-depression. I'm supposed to forget about my apprehension of my new challenges and just get over it? Seriously???

I have now adapted a revision of this advice to: "Work Through It."

It's similar to driving through a torrential rain storm. Sometimes you just have to slow down, process it, work it through, accept it and then, slowly...move forward.

Questions to Process:
- What do you BELIEVE happened?
- What ACTUALLY happened?
- What did you contribute to what happened?
- What would you do differently, if you could?
- Who hurt you?
- Who did you hurt?

- Have you asked for forgiveness?
- Have you forgiven yourself?

Here are a few valuable quotes:
"No one can make you feel inferior without your consent." - Eleanor Roosevelt

"The first time you make a mistake it's an accident. The second time you make the same mistake, it's on purpose, and the third time you make the same mistake, it's no longer a mistake, it's a habit." - unknown

An article I found gave these helpful tips:

1. *Feel the pain*
Hiding your feelings or pretending that everything is okay will get you nowhere on the path toward healing. You've got to let it out. Get mad if you're angry. Cry if you're hurt. If you feel like you could just scream, do it. Keeping it all bottled up inside will result in bitterness and depression; it can turn a one-time offense into a lifetime disposition.

2. *Talk about it*
Find a trusted friend or two and vent. An outside perspective may help you sort out your feelings. At the very least, it's someone to sympathize with you and hold your hand.

3. *Be wary of seeking closure*
I think closure is over-rated. Despite how much your bruised ego thirsts for it, trying to figure out what went wrong and who did what will not help. Trust me, you don't really want to know why someone rejected you. It's like running back into a burning house to find out how the fire started. It's far too difficult to find the source, and you will inevitably get burned in the process. Just walk away.

4. *Embrace your new normal*
Sometimes disappointments come with a major change. Divorce, loss of a job and such alter your day-to-day life. Things simply aren't the way they used to be.

Part of getting over the past is being fully in the present. You may have lost something, but you've also created space in your life for something new to come along. Instead of pining for what used to be, enjoy what's here now and look forward to what's to come.

5. *Give it time*

If you broke your leg, you wouldn't expect to wake up the next day, whip off the cast and start running. It takes time to heal. So goes the heart. Give yourself time to recover. Know that things will get better and a day will come when the pain you feel today is a distance memory.

http://www.beliefnet.com/Health/Emotional-Health/5-Ways-to-Get-Over-It.aspx?b=1

I now know when I have finally "Worked Through It": When I finally reach the stage that I can think of the other person or the situation…wish them well…and feel peace…I know I am ready to MOVE ON.

Are You?....

8
"The Way We Were..."

Most of us remember that iconic movie with Robert Redford and Barbra Streisand in 1973 called "The Way We Were."
Barbara Streisand even sang the soundtrack of the movie. Some of the lyrics are:

Memories, light the corners of my mind

Misty watercolor memories of the way we were.

Scattered pictures of the smiles we left behind

smiles we give to one another

for the way we were.

Can it be that it was all so simple then

or has time rewritten every line?

If we had the chance to do it all again

tell me would we? Could we?

Memories, may be beautiful and yet

what's too painful to remember

we simply choose to forget

So it's the laughter we will remember

whenever we remember

the way we were.

http://www.metrolyrics.com/the-way-we-were-lyrics-barbara-streisand.html

As I reflect on this song, I think about everyone I have ever met in my life. Many were blessings…some were lessons.

To celebrate its 10th Anniversary, Facebook allowed an option called "A Look Back." It constructed a 1-minute video of you, based on your history with Facebook. As I watched many of these, I realized that a lot of feelings I had of most of my family and friends were of "The Way They Were…"

Time passes…we change…whether in age, perspective, goals or health. We often set ourselves up for disappointment when we judge people by how they WERE instead of how they ARE now.

We don't expect anyone or anything else to change…all the while, we are changing every day ourselves.

So…how do I reconcile this?

I choose to be thankful for what great things and qualities are still the same…feel blessed for experiencing what was in the past…and understand that they may never be again…

Memories…

9
Searching for Ranch Dressing

I woke up at 3:35 a.m. one morning, highly annoyed. It all stemmed from a vivid dream I had. It went something like this:

I am sitting at one of the front-row, reserved tables at an elegant luncheon. I am here to receive the coveted Distinguished Service Award in the presence of approximately 1,000 individuals and dignitaries.

I am dressed in a crisp linen, khaki pants suit, with a springtime floral blouse and comfortable but fashionable three-inch, burgundy heels.

As I sit at my table, alone, before the guests arrive, I decide to proceed with eating my salad, which has been pre-set on the beautifully, decorated tables. I don't like to speak immediately after eating.

Placed in front of me is a very eye-pleasing salad. It has mixed greens, grape tomatoes, multi-colored peppers, cucumbers, mushrooms and a sprinkling of pine nuts. I love colorful food!

I bless my food and reach for the salad dressing. I have a strong desire for Ranch Dressing. I see a silver dressing container that has Balsamic Vinaigrette. Although I like it, my taste buds are dead-set on Ranch Dressing.

I politely ask the waiter for Ranch Dressing, preferably Low Fat or Light. He says he will oblige. After about 5 minutes, I am growing slowly anxious. I want to eat my salad so I can enjoy it and be nicely digested before the attendees arrive. I like plenty of dressing on my salad.

I stop another waiter and ask him for my Ranch Dressing. He apologizes for the tardiness of the other waiter and moves with a sense of urgency to fulfill my request.

Another 5 minutes pass and still…no Ranch Dressing. Needless to say, anticipation and a tad bit of nervousness begin to kick in. My patience is wearing thin.

I ever so subtly go to the back service area door, waiting for the next waiter or the manager to appear. After about 5 minutes, the Service Manager comes out. With extreme patience and bridled irritation, I explain to the manager my dilemma. I tell him that I am an Award Recipient that has requested twice simply for some Ranch Dressing, preferably Low Fat or Light.

He apologizes profusely and insists that he will bring it to my table himself. I return quietly to my seat, pleased that my "salad dressing" issue has been resolved. I quietly concentrate on my acceptance speech.

However, another 5 minutes pass and still…no Ranch Dressing. My irritation has exceeded my patience limit. I quietly, but sternly, go to the Service Door again.

After a few moments of no-one-coming-out, I enter.

Having to do this much unnecessary walking in heels was yet another source of my growing aggravation. I proceed down a dimmed hallway to the service kitchen. I stand there in amazement!

There are approximately 75 servers, all doing their jobs serving the audience what appears to be a very lovely, delectable meal. Nevertheless, one of them cannot simply bring me my requested Ranch Dressing???

I approach the first 5 servers. They look shocked! Their faces reflect a response of, *"What is a guest doing back here?!!"*

I ask, in as calm and non-annoyed voice as I can possibly muster, *"May I please have some Ranch Dressing, preferably Low Fat or Light?"*

No one responds. They all look at me, somewhat confused. I state my request again, a bit more firmly this time, *"I would like some Ranch Dressing, Please?!"*

Still no response. I then notice that they are all Hispanic. Finally, one meek gentleman says, *"No Hablo Inglés."*

I am now at to the end of my patience point. I announce, somewhat loudly, "*Does anyone here speak English?!"*

Abruptly, the Service Manager, whom I had been waiting for 10 minutes ago, steps out of his office to see what the commotion is all about. He approaches me with a very embarrassed, red face. *"Madame, may I help you?"*

I state, *"Uhm, like you were supposed to have helped me 10 minutes ago by bringing me my Ranch Dressing?!"*

He states, *"My humble apologies...I had delegated that task to be taken care of."*

"Well, it has not been!" I shout, uncontrollably upset at this point. *"I am an Award Recipient! I simply requested Ranch Dressing so that I could eat my salad before the ceremony! Is this too much to ask?!"*

Although the Service Manager tries to immediately get the Ranch Dressing himself and calm me down, he is too late. I am so frustrated, that I storm out and trudge back down the long corridor, fuming! My feet are beginning to get a little achy…

Oh, well….I finally compose myself and take a deep, cleansing breathe…..the salad will just have to wait. I have an Award to receive!

As I near the Service Door, I hear the Master of Ceremonies, say:

"Her kindness, patience and tireless efforts in our community make this award most fitting. I am honored this afternoon to present the Distinguished Service Award to Janette McGowen!!"

(APPLAUSE)

"Unfortunately, Janette was here earlier, but had to leave. I gladly accept this award on her behalf. Thank you all for your attendance and make it a great afternoon."

I just stand there at that door…in complete shock!

I am too embarrassed and humiliated to go in until I see that all of the attendees have left the dining room. I quietly return to my table. My complete meal, including dessert, is still there, patiently waiting for me. I sit down, put the napkin in my lap, bless my food again and reach for the dressing that is at the table.

Sitting right in front of me… is a new, silver cup full of Ranch Dressing.

Uhm…I wonder if the dessert is a piece of "Humble Pie"….

10
"Living a Long Life or a Life Well-Lived..."

"Some people live a long life. Others live a life well-lived.' This was stated by my minister, Bro. David Jones, Jr. during a eulogy he gave. It was for a 37-year-old son, father, Christian and friend to many. He died tragically in an accident on his job.

With close to 2,000 people in attendance at the funeral, it was obvious that he was a well-loved and admired human being who gave so much of himself to others.

As I reflected on Bro. Jones' words, I realized that many of us never think about our own mortality.

As Christians, we know it is God's Plan for us all to cross the "Finish Line" of this existence, called Death, in order to be with HIM in Heaven for eternity. Satan loves to make us think we are meant to live forever and to fear death.

I now realize that funerals are for those of us who are still here.

Question: **Have you ever wondered what your funeral will look like?**

How many people's lives have you so-positively impacted that they will grieve your absence?

LIFE is truly NOT about:

- How many sales you made;
- How many "friends" you have;
- How many famous people you have met;
- Promotions you earned;
- Raises you received;
- How big and nice your house is;

- New cars you bought;
- Designer purses and clothes you own;
- Performances you gave;
- Hit Songs you sang;
- How much weight you lost;
- Awards you received.

These things are for YOURSELF.

When I see the latest escapades of entertainers like Miley Cyrus or Justin Bieber, I quietly think sadly to myself, "God has blessed them both with talent and international exposure to help others. Satan has a grip on them, making them believe they are invincible and their lives are "All About Them.'"

I pray that we all come to the realization soon that God expects us to use the "gifts" he has given each and every one of us to GLORIFY HIM and to help others.

What will people say about you? What do you want your legacy to be?

Is your life making a difference or are you just living "the good life?"

Actually…it's the small things you do that can positively impact other's lives. Simple, private gestures include:

- A smile,
- A hug or a pat on the back,
- A kind word,
- Helping someone to LOL! (Laugh Out Loud),
- Paying for someone's meal at a restaurant or a drive-through window,
- Sending someone a greeting card,

- Stop talking and just LISTEN,
- Praying deeply and deliberately for someone,
- Giving someone a compliment,
- Holding the door open for someone,
- Giving an elderly or disabled person your seat on a bus or train,
- Anonymously donating to a food bank, mission, or homeless shelter—other than during Thanksgiving or Christmas.

Matthew 6:3-4 (NKJV) says that *"what charitable deeds you do secretly; God sees secretly and will reward you openly."*

We should change our focus from "impressing man" to "impressing GOD."

Are you striving to live "a long life or a life well-lived?"...

11
The Prodigal Son's Brother

Do you ever feel as though you are doing everything the Lord wants you to do and HE does not seem to notice?

- You follow the Ten Commandments.
- You strive to live a decent, moral life.
- You don't drink, do drugs or use profanity.
- You strive to be a good steward of your resources.
- You are always generous and helping others.

Yet, you constantly see people who live atrocious, sinful, dreadful lives and appear to be rewarded for it…even blessed.

I have followed the media coverage of celebrities who have made horrible mistakes in their lives, i.e., Tiger Woods, Michael Vick, Robert Downey, Jr. and Lindsey Lohan. More recently are Miley Cyrus and Justin Bieber. They are allowed to "come to their senses" and appear to be celebrated and blessed.

What about those of us who are obedient? It almost appears that we are being penalized for doing the right thing.

Reflect on Luke 15:11-32 (NIV), the Parable of the Lost (Prodigal) Son:

Think about the Prodigal Son's Brother. He spent his life being obedient to his father. Yet, his younger brother asks for his inheritance so he can go out into the world. His father gives it to him. He leaves to live a life of worldly exploits. He eventually squanders it all. He ends up working in a pig field. He finally comes to his senses and realizes that even his father's servants live a better life than he does right now in the mud among the swine. He returns home to apologize to his father and agree to be a servant.

His father sees him approaching and rejoices. The young son tells his father he has sinned against him and does not deserve to be his son. Nevertheless, his father embraces him! He has his servants bring him a robe, a ring for his finger and sandals for his feet. He commands that their fattest calf be offered. He orders a feast of celebration.

Needless to say, the older brother is upset and refuses to go to the celebration. When the Father goes to him to ask him to come, he angrily asks, "Why are you rewarding my younger brother for disobedience? I have been obedient to you the whole time. Yet, you never gave me a young goat or hosted a feast of celebration for me?"

Luke 15:31-32 (NIV) says, *'My son,' the father said, 'you are always with me, and everything I have is yours. But we had to celebrate and be glad, because this brother of yours was dead and is alive again; he was lost and is found.'*

How do you keep yourself from feeling bitter like The Prodigal Son's Brother?

A similar instance is revealed when The Lord speaks about the Lost Sheep in Matthew 18:11-14 (NKJV) He says, *"For the Son of Man has come to save that which was lost. What do you think? If a man has a hundred sheep, and one of them goes astray, does he not leave the ninety-nine and go to the mountains to seek the one that is straying? And if he should find it, assuredly, I say to you, he rejoices more over that sheep than over the ninety-nine that did not go astray. Even so it is not the will of your Father who is in heaven that one of these little ones should perish."*

Why would he abandon 99 sheep just to go find one that had strayed? Do you think the 99 sheep were a little upset?

They may have thought, "Here we are, being obedient, following the Shepherd. Yet, you drop everything to go find that one sheep that has gotten lost. And you rejoice when you find him? What's up with that?"

What Can We Do To Alleviate Our Concerns?

We must embrace a few basic principles:

The Lord Came to Save the Sinners

We first must understand Matthew 9:13 (KJV) as the Lord proclaimed, *"But go ye and learn what that meaneth, I will have mercy, and not sacrifice: for I am not come to call the righteous, but sinners to repentance."*

Jesus would not have had to die on the cross if everyone was already righteous and obedient. He died for the sinners to be forgiven. Just as he stated regarding the Lost Sheep in Matthew 18:11 (KJV), *"For the Son of man is come to save that which was lost."*

I somewhat relate this to being a child and getting jealous that my parents were focused on my sibling's bad behavior and didn't seem to notice my good behavior. Now, with wisdom, I understand that just because they were focused on correcting the bad behavior and even celebrating when it became good, did not mean that they didn't notice, appreciate and actually reward my consistent, good behavior.

Stay In Your Own Lane

We must take our focus on what God appears to be doing in others' lives and focus on 100% obedience to HIM in your own life.

God has the creation of the heavens, the earth, and our existence on it as part of HIS Divine Master Plan. It may not make sense to you, but it makes perfect sense to Our Loving Creator.

Romans 8:28 (KJV) states *"And we know that all things work together for good to them that love God, to them who are the called according to his purpose."*

We must stop trying to "rationalize" things in our minds. Isaiah 55:8-9 (NIV) says, *"For my thoughts are not your thoughts, neither are your ways my ways," declares the LORD. "As the heavens are higher than the earth, so are my ways higher than your ways and my thoughts than your thoughts."*

Maintain or Renew Your Faith:

When we question God regarding issues like this, we have to remember what He said in Matthew 17:20 (NIV), *"Because you have so little faith. Truly I tell you, if you have faith as small as a mustard seed, you can say to this mountain, 'Move from here to there,' and it will move. Nothing will be impossible for you."*

Hebrews 11:6 (KJV) says, *"But without faith it is impossible to please him: for he that cometh to God must believe that he is, and that he is a rewarder of them that diligently seek him."*

We have to TRUST Him. Proverbs 3:5-6 (KJV) says, *"Trust in the LORD with all thine heart; and lean not unto thine own understanding. In all thy ways acknowledge him, and he shall direct thy paths."*

Your Obedience is NOT going Unnoticed:

The Prodigal Son's Father told his upset, older son in Luke 15:31 (NIV) *'My son,' the father said, 'you are always with me, and everything I have is yours.'*

He was trying to explain to his son that his obedience is always recognized and will ultimately be rewarded.

When we are 100% focused on being obedient to God, He sees it. He reiterates this in Matthew 6:4 (KJV) *"... and thy Father which seeth in secret himself shall reward thee openly."*

Allow GOD to USE You:
The challenge that we face is to stay focused and remain obedient, no matter what we see or hear. James 4:10 (KJV) states *"Humble yourselves in the sight of the Lord, and he shall lift you up."*

God has a divine purpose for your life. Your life does not belong to you. Jesus Christ paid for your life by His crucifixion. If we would only surrender and humble ourselves, then this would allow God to use us. He is trying to use your quiet obedience as a public testimony to others.

Don't get angry or frustrated like The Prodigal Son's Brother. Stay Faithful and Obedient.

It Is Not Going Unnoticed By God...

This reflection was awarded an "Honorable Mention" in the Inspirational Writing category in the 80TH Annual Writer's Digest Writing Competition

12
"Thrill of Victory - Agony of Defeat"

Many of us remember hearing this phrase during the Olympics.

Unfortunately, we are becoming a nation teaching our children that "there are no losers."

Guess What? Yes, There Are!

I saw a Facebook post of a parent boasting of their child's "4th Place Finish" in a competition. Unfortunately, this world does not reward effort or intention. It only rewards WINNERS.

As parents and supporters, it is appropriate to encourage kids for their efforts. But, we must help them understand that, with more focus, practice and effort, they can eventually WIN.

If we continue to reward "less than excellence," we are crippling others to be competitive in the "real world." Allowing your children to believe that "everyone is a winner" is setting them up for devastation in life.

When I was growing up, (I was born in 1964 – the end of the Baby Boomer era), I was a "tomboy" at heart. I was, and am still, competitive.

I participated in softball and basketball, as well as competed in 4-H.

In every competition, there was that coveted "1st Place Prize." There were WINNERS and LOSERS.

This is evident in the workplace I remember, in my early career in Sales, winning "Top Sales Person of the Month." I was awarded a nice bonus and got to park in a reserved parking space for the month. Guess What? There were no bonuses or reserved parking spaces for 2nd, 3rd, or 4th place.

I am intrigued when I watch the Kentucky Derby. The coveted horse may win "by a nose." That fraction of a second is the difference between winning $1.4 million dollars and in the Winner's Circle, and winning $400,000 in 2nd place; $200,000 in 3rd place; $100,000 in 4th place; $60,000 in 5th place and not being heard of again.
http://bleacherreport.com/articles/2051805-kentucky-derby-2014-prize-money-full-purse-info-for-winners-at-churchill-downs

I have watched the Golden Globes, the Tony Awards, the Academy Awards and the Emmy Awards. In each category, although there were several nominees, they had (1) Winner. Afterward, the press was not flocking after the nominees – only the Winners.

Case in Point:

This is evident in watching the 2014 Winter Olympics in Sochi, Russia. The USA struggled in the medal count. Specifically, I watched the Snowboarding Competition. USA's Shaun White, assured to be a Gold Medalist or at least a Medal contender – came in 4th Place! And guess what? HE LOST! No Gold, Silver or Bronze Medal. No standing up on the podium.

However, I was warmed by his genuine humility. He sincerely congratulated the Gold Medal Winner. When interviewed, he simply stated, "I just didn't have my best day today." We must teach our children to be humble in both victory and defeat.

"You don't truly appreciate the THRILL OF VICTORY if you have not suffered the AGONY OF DEFEAT." – Janette McGowen

I grew up proud that the United States of America was #1 in the world (for apparently everything.) We were considered a "Super Power" on the international arena.

That status seems to be eroding. While we, as Americans, have our "noses up in the air" arrogantly and with greed, other countries are quietly and deliberately "getting it done." Yes…their methods may seem extreme to us, but the results are without question.

I know personally, I am thankful for the "Agony of Defeat." This has made me reassess, make corrections and keep striving. This has helped me truly enjoy and savor in the "Thrill of Victory."

There is no such thing as "everyone is a winner." There is only (1).

I plan on it being me ☺….

13
I Need You, My Friend…

I woke up suddenly one evening, very anxious and restless. I found out that a dear friend had collapsed Sunday morning as he was about to enter worship service. He had to be rushed to the hospital and was in Intensive Care. I prayed for him throughout the night and into the next day…and continued "praying without ceasing."

I finally woke up at 2:00 a.m., inspired to write this.

Dealing with health challenges of my own, as well as attending a funeral of a young man recently, has truly humbled me and heightened my need to tell people I care about how I feel about them right NOW. Tomorrow is not promised to any of us.

Here is what I was compelled to say:

"My Friend"
by Janette McGowen

I need you here, My Friend…

I need to grow old with you…

I need to witness you walking your daughter down the aisle…

I need to see you holding your first grandchild…

I need to see you accomplish your Heart's Desire…

I need to be able to see your dimples and your shy smile…

I need to hear your firm reprimand and stern encouragement…

I need to giggle at your impatience and my ability to annoy you to no end…

I need you to roll your eyes with embarrassment at my extreme sentimentality…

I pray for you, more than I pray for myself…

Please don't leave me now…

I Need You, My Friend...

14
Heavenly-Minded or Earthly-Good?

I remember when I was with my first company, straight out of college. I had entered Sales and had been quite successful over the years.

One year, my company decided to renovate our cubicles. We were to work from home for a few weeks. This was great! I pulled my car to the front of the building and made numerous trips with boxes.

It was on a Wednesday. I was diligent about packing up my office. I figured I could finish by 5:00 p.m., make it home, unpack, freshen up and make it across town to Bible Study by 7:00 p.m.

On my initial trip to my car, I noticed a young lady sitting in the lobby. It appeared as though she was off-work, waiting for someone. She appeared anxious. Although I DID see her, I was busy at the task at hand.

(Note: My personality is one in which I tend to "know everyone.") Each trip, I chatted and laughed with everyone from other colleagues to managers to the Security staff.

Each trip, I noticed her…**watching me**. I felt a little pride to display that I knew a lot of employees.

I was completing my final trip to my car. I was so proud of myself! I was right on schedule. As I was telling the Security Staff good-bye, the young lady approached me. She said, *"Excuse me. I work in the Call Center. I see that you are leaving. May I ask you for a favor?"* I always liked to believe that I was the Ultimate Problem-Solver. I replied. "Sure!"

She humbly asked, almost whispered, *"Would it be possible for you to give me a ride home?"* I was shocked! She continued, *"My family just relocated here from another state a few months ago. My brother was supposed to pick me up, but he called. He has been in a minor car accident. He has our only car. I'm not sure when he can make it here."* I asked, "What time did you get off work?" She said, *"2:30 p.m."* Wow! She had been waiting for 2 ½ hours! **Ugh!! She is going to make me late for BIBLE STUDY!!!**

I finally agreed to take her home. I made sure that Security saw her leaving with me. **(In my mind, I am still thinking, "I can still keep my schedule and make it to CHURCH.")** I asked her where she lived. She said, *"Franklin, Tennessee. Off of Mack Hatcher Parkway."* **(Quietly, I scream, "Are you kidding me?!!" Traffic is a nightmare in that direction this time of day! It was the opposite direction from where I lived!)**

When we got in the car, I secretly put a pair of scissors under my driver's seat for protection. She initially appeared guarded and shy, virtually hugging the passenger door. However, while driving on the interstate, she became more relaxed and began talking. She said, *"I have never asked anyone for a ride before. I thought you may be an Axe Murderer or a Serial Killer. But, you seemed so nice…like you knew everybody. And I figured, if Security knew you, you were probably safe."*

After about 1 hour of rush-hour-traffic, I pulled up in front of her home. Her Mom was ecstatic! She looked up at the sky, offering her thanks for answered prayers and waved to me with sincere gratitude. The young lady was smiling and so thankful. I gave her my business card and said, *"**I work up on the 3rd floor in Sales. If you ever need a ride or anything, please give me a call.**"*

I made it home at 7:35 p.m. Yes…I was too late to make it across town to Bible Study.

What a profound lesson! I was so busy trying to "get to Bible Study," that I almost missed the opportunity to put my learning into action.

Be careful of being so *"Heavenly-Minded"* **that you are of no** *"Earthly-Good"*…

15
The Other Shoe

While in the midst of my emerging professional career in 1998, the media was blazing over the scandal of President Bill Clinton and a 22-year-old White House Intern, Monica Lewinsky.

Although I felt this was a shocking and unfortunate lapse in moral judgment by President Clinton, I think I was more appalled by the **hypocrisy** of the people leading the charge to impeach him.

Example: *"Speaker of the House Newt Gingrich, Representative from Georgia and leader of the Republican Revolution of 1994, admitted in 1998 to having had an affair with a House intern while he was married to his second wife, at the same time as he was leading the impeachment of Bill Clinton for perjury regarding an affair with intern Monica Lewinsky."*
http://en.wikipedia.org/wiki/Lewinsky_scandal

A co-worker was "going ballistic" about the situation. Emphatically, she ranted, "What kind of role model is he?! What am I supposed to tell my kids?!" The more upset she became, the calmer I became. She finally stopped and asked, "Why aren't you saying anything? Aren't you upset, too?" I paused and replied, "Well...first of all, President Clinton should not be our role model. Jesus Christ is. Secondly, I think this is a powerful example for your kids. They see a human being make a mistake and lie about it (like most of us do.) He was "found out." He had to confess his sin and ask for forgiveness. However, he had to do this in front of the nation. It really is a test of OUR ability to forgive."

As I was spending some quiet time during my lunch hour one day, these words and phrases starting overwhelming me. I felt as though I was simply a *"transcriber for my spirit."* I never considered myself a poet. While writing, even the title emerged.

Here is the result:

"The Other Shoe"

by Janette McGowen

When the friend needs befriending,

And the comforter needs comforting,

When the Savior now needs saving;

The attacker is attacked,

The accuser is now the accused,

And the behaved one is now misbehaving.

When the forgiver needs forgiving,

The caregiver needs caring for,

And the nurse now needs to be nursed;

The lover needs loving,

The employer is now unemployed,

And ironically, this was all unrehearsed.

When the disciplinarian needs discipline,

The trustee can no longer be trusted,

And the painter is now being painted;

When the home builder needs a house,

The married one now has no spouse,

And what was truth now seems tainted.

Whatever someone does to you,

Without forgiveness,

you do right back to them;

And guess what? No one wins,

The world runs amuck,

And all seems gloomy and dim.

Oh, how we go through our lives, not noticing a thing,

With our possessions and our status and our lists;

And with a quick turn of fate,

We find everything in our lives,

No longer truly exists.

Oh, how small, yet connected, we find the world can be,

Amazing, yet so brutally true;

When we find our one foot, that was always secure,

Now Resting in The Other Shoe...

16
FORGIVE While...Remembering???

We are often given the advice to *"Forgive and Forget."*

Merriam-Webster defines these words as:

Forgive: to stop feeling anger toward (someone who has done something wrong): to stop blaming (someone) :to stop feeling anger about (something) :to forgive someone for (something wrong) http://www.merriam-webster.com/dictionary/forgive

Forget: to be unable to think of or remember (something) :to stop thinking or caring about : to cease from doing :to disregard intentionally :to give up hope for or expectation of :to cease remembering or noticing. http://www.merriam-webster.com/dictionary/forget

I have found it difficult to reconcile this advice. I can forgive; but, if I forget, will I be vulnerable to this happening to me again?

Case in Point: People of Jewish descent. They have forgiven the Hitler regime for the atrocities done to them and their ancestors during the Holocaust. However, Jewish children are taught about the Holocaust at a very early age. Their rationale is that "what is forgotten can be repeated."
http://www.kveller.com/preschooler/How_To_Talk_About/holocaust-talking-to-kids.shtml

"As the Nobel laureate Elie Wiesel warned years ago, to forget a holocaust is to kill twice." — Iris Chang, The Rape of Nanking

Although I don't closely adhere to Zodiac Signs, I am Taurus, the Bull. One of our characteristics is that we are *very loyal. But once that trust is breached, it is virtually impossible to earn back.*

In my early professional career, I lowered my defenses and trusted a colleague who I believed to be a dear friend and confidante' for almost 9 years – all throughout my naïve' 20's. Although **"2+2 never quite added up to 4,"** I ignored these red flags. I was profoundly loyal. I trusted her completely and unconditionally, going out of my way to do any and everything in the world for her.

When an intervention occurred of other friends trying to enlighten me, I still refused to believe them. It took them repeating to me things she had told them very freely – my most intimate, embarrassing secrets that I had only ever told her – for me to have my eyes opened. I practically hyperventilated! I felt as though someone had literally punched me in the stomach – leaving me unable to breathe. This ultimate betrayal was overwhelming. I was inconsolable…

I am sad to say that my erratic response, although very effective and masterfully executed, was not reflective of my authentic self. I remember being upset with someone, who reminded me of Matthew 18:15 by saying, *"You really should have went to her, and her alone."* I emotionally rejected this advice. I regretfully wish I hadn't.

Lesson Learned: *"When someone does something wrong to you, without forgiveness, you become them."* – Dr. David Jones, Jr.

Nevertheless, I still have lasting scars of remembrance. Trusting others now is very difficult. The endearing term "friend" is used very cautiously.

I ended up working with the colleague again years later, as well as crossing paths at a few social events. Will I ever trust her again? Unlikely. Although I still remember the hurt and betrayal I endured, I was and am, even now, able to think of her fondly and wish her well.

One of the most memorable lines in the Tyler Perry movie, *Diary of a Mad Black Woman*, is when Madea gives advice to her domestically-abused niece, Helen:

"You think you over something? You think you're ready to get on with your life? This is how you really find out if you're over someone: If you get the opportunity to get even with someone and you don't take it, then you're over it…"
http://jusbreathe-magically.blogspot.com/2008/07/diary-of-mad-black-woman.html

Powerful Quotes to Remind You:

"Life becomes easier when you learn to accept the apology you never got." – Robert Brault

"Forgive your enemies, but never forget their names." – John F. Kennedy

"Forgiveness does not always lead to a healed relationship. Some people are not capable of love, and it might be wise to let them go, along with your anger. Just wish them well and take care of yourself." – unknown

"To forgive is to set a prisoner free and discover that the prisoner was you." – Lewis Smedes

"Forgiveness is giving up the hope that the past could have been any different. It's accepting the past for what it was, and using this time and this moment to help yourself move forward." – Oprah Winfrey

"Forgive them, even if they are not sorry. Holding onto anger only hurts you, not them." – unknown

"When tempted to 'Fight Fire with Fire', remember that the Fire Department usually uses water." – unknown

"True Forgiveness is when you can say, 'Thank You for that Experience.'" – Oprah Winfrey

I Challenge You to *"Forgive while Remembering,"* Accept the Lessons Learned, Forgive Yourself and Move Forward…

17
"Are You TOO BUSY???"

I recall someone, whose opinion I respect and value, telling me that although they were proud of me, asking me to discontinue sending them my blog posts because they were "too busy" to read them.

How can someone say they care about you, say that you are talented...but can't give "3 minutes" of their day to read a blog or to be supportive?

Although I immediately adhered to this request, it forced me to reflect on my own "busyness."

I have to humbly admit that I have been guilty of this. Telling people that I was too busy to talk; too busy to read and reply to their voicemail, text or email; too busy to do lunch. *Interesting...how we find time to do what is important to us...*

Try This:

- Make a list of all things you are "Too Busy" doing.
- If you drop-dead right now, *Will They Matter?*

Guess What?...Life will move right on without you.

And the things you were "Too Busy" doing?
Either someone else will do them – or they will be deemed *nonessential* and ignored.

If we are "too busy" to love and encourage each other...then what's the point of our existence?

Parents? If you are "too busy":
- to read to your children;
- to cheer them on;

- to be interested in their opinions, hopes and dreams;
- to support them in their goals and endeavors;
- to LISTEN to them;
- to tell them you LOVE them.

You are busier than GOD meant for you to be.

God gives us millions of ways each day to do HIS WILL, which is to love and care about each other.

Powerful Quotes to Live By:

"No matter how 'BUSY' a person is, if they really care, they will always find the time for you." – unknown

"Never get so busy making a living that you forget to make a life." – unknown

"It's not enough to be busy, so are ants. The question is, what are we busy about?" -Henry David Thoreau

"Stop the glorification of busy." – unknown

"It's not about having time. It's about MAKING time." - unknown

We ALL are given a set time per day: 86,400 Seconds; 1,440 Minutes and 24 Hours in a Day. How are we using them?

"Being Busy" is a powerful tool used by Satan to keep you distracted from GOD. Are you allowing Satan to win?

Are You "Too Busy?"

18
Fading into Obscurity...
(my most personal, raw, scary, & revealing reflection yet...)

Merriam-Webster defines "Obscurity" as : the state of being unknown or forgotten. http://www.merriam-webster.com/dictionary/obscurity

In the past, I was somewhat of an "extrovert," who loved meeting new people. Achieving an Advanced Toastmaster certification has resulted in speaking opportunities with audiences as large as 1,000 people, handled fearlessly. My professional background is in Sales. Presentations? No problem. I realized that I have the gift of establishing "instant rapport" and gaining trust. I was "Ms. Independent" and a total Control Freak.

I absolutely loved serving at my church – from being my minister's loyal Staff Assistant to being a reliable, valuable resource to our leadership, office administration, assistant ministers, and 50+ ministries.

I took the "lead" when it came to family activities. I was a "Mover and Shaker" and loved *"being in the know."*

Funny, what an unexpected, devastating health diagnosis can do. It's as though my life came to a "screeching halt."

I was diagnosed with Primary Progressive Multiple Sclerosis two years ago. It has taken me this long to even say it or write about it without breaking-down crying. (OK???...Getting there...*as tears roll down my face...*)

My minister helped me realize that I am experiencing the "Stages of Grief." I am grieving the "death" or the end of my life, as I knew it. I am still suppressing anger, bargaining with God, resenting and not-yet-fully-accepting having to adjust to adapt to this "New Normal."

I was told by an MS Counselor that: Cognitively and Logistically – I appear to have it all together. However, Emotionally?? I seem to be struggling…

And then to tops things off…my employer eliminated my entire national division. I am now unemployed…

Being forced to "be still" has been very revealing. I NOW see that everything that I was "so busy" doing…everyone that I thought relied on me…everything that I was so "obsessed about"…is moving right along…without me…without my involvement or my input.

I am feeling as though I am *"no longer relevant"*…

I had an **"Aha Moment"** during the Tennessee Titans' 2013 Football season. I identified with Jake Locker, the Quarterback. He was so used to Coach Mike Munchak relying on him for game strategy and team leadership. But after his injuries…he realized that he was no longer "on the field" or even "in the game." Although Coach Munchak respected him and what he had brought to the team in the past, he no longer needed to confer with him on the sidelines. Games still needed to be won…Playoffs need to be earned…the Super Bowl goal still needed to be met. WOW!…what a "light bulb" moment…

I have been trying to retreat…similar to a turtle pulling its head back into its shell. Words like "Joy, Happiness, and Fun" are somewhat elusive to me. I have become quiet; less opinionated; less confident; more evasive; more reclusive and less participatory. I find that I am even dressing in subtle, non-attention-drawing clothes. Please, let me just ease into the background…out-of-sight-out-of-mind, behind-the-curtains, in the darkness, invisible…

I am trying to *"Fade into Obscurity."*

But, apparently, GOD has other plans for me. You See?...HE Won't Let Me!!!

I thought I could simply "hide" behind my computer and my own personal journal.

However, it is as though HE has gently "nudged" me forward via blogging.

Blogging has pushed me into writing (something I have always loved to do – but never had time to pursue.) *I am humbled that my blog seems to have resonated with so many people.*

For the first time in my life, I feel that I am truly learning to "surrender" and really TRUST GOD.

It's as though I am floating along in a row boat…

Can't Swim…
No Life Jacket…
No Oars…
No Compass…

Just Floating out into the abyss…toward that endless horizon…
I hear one of my favorite scriptures speaking to me. Proverbs 3:5-6 (NKJV): *"Trust in the Lord with all your heart, And lean not on your own understanding; In all your ways acknowledge Him, And He shall direct your paths."*

I must allow the LORD to direct my path, chart my course and determine my destination. I don't know where I am going. I will just sit back and enjoy the journey…

Feel Free to Join Me…

19
"No Matter Where You Go – There You Are"

A gentleman posted on Facebook his decision to move his membership to another church. The reason he gave was that he wanted to worship at a church *"where I feel accepted, loved and not judged…"*

The humble question: *If you want to feel acceptance, were you accepting of others? If you wanted to feel love and non-judgment, did you give love and non-judgment?* (Honestly, over the years that I've known him, the impression he radiated was one of appearing unloving, judgmental and unapproachable...)

Another friend asked my advice regarding relationships following her third divorce. I asked her if she wanted me to tell her what she wanted to hear or my honest observation. She insisted she wanted straight-talk. I calmly replied, *"Well, your ex-spouses have moved on to have happy marriages and families. Unfortunately, the only common denominator between all three relationships…is YOU."*

I know colleagues who "job-hopped" to new cities. In each new job, they had the same complaints: *"the culture was wrong; management was unfair; the other associates were unprofessional; the city is congested; the people are rude..."*

What they failed to realize is that going somewhere else is only GEOGRAPHY. **You take You with You.** Often, the biggest change we need to make is not in our location – but in our thoughts and attitudes.

A few tough questions to ask include:

IF I want to be loved…am I loving?
IF I want friends…am I friendly?
IF I want people to feel comfortable approaching me…am I approachable?

Sometimes, we need to "mentally" step outside of ourselves to see ourselves. We can only grow if we are "brutally honest" with ourselves and see things as they ARE, not as we'd like to see them. We are often guilty of making excuses such as:

"The church didn't make me feel welcome."

"My husband didn't make me happy."

"I didn't get anything out of worship service today."

"I didn't get anything out of that meeting."

Another example would be if you were a habitual smoker, yet complained because everywhere you went, it smelled like smoke.

One of my favorite quotes is: *"We are often preaching to others to get out of the rain, while others are looking at you quite confused…because you are the only one dripping wet…"* unknown

We often measure things in life by what we **didn't** receive. The question is: What did you give?

"Be the Change You Wish to See In The World." - Mahatma Gandhi

Until you deal with the ***"person reflecting back to you in the mirror,"*** **everywhere you go is going to eventually look like the place you left.**

"If you change the way you look at things, the things you look at change." - Wayne Dyer

The best conclusion we could ever hope for is quoted by T.S. Eliot:

"We shall not cease from exploration
And the end of all our exploring
Will be to arrive where we started
And know the place for the first time."

20
Answers to Our Prayers

How many of you have actually *"prayed on your knees"* or *"knelt in prayer?"* We sing songs about it. We use it in our clichés. Have you actually done it? It's a position of humility. Prayer is a PRIVATE conversation with you and God.

Most people use this time to ask for things? Guess What?

GOD is not Santa Claus!

Santa Claus is a legend of historical fiction. He is make-believe. GOD is our Creator. HE is Real.

Oftentimes, when we pray, we don't like the answer we get.

Sometimes it is: **Yes**

Sometimes it is: **No**

Sometimes it is: **Not Now.**

Regardless, we have to thank HIM anyway and accept the answer.

If the answer is **Yes**…give thanks for answered prayers.

If the answer is **No**…it may mean that it is not in your best interest or part of God's Master Plan.

If the answer is **Not Now**…it may mean *"be patient. I have something better in store for you."*

God is your "Most Trusted Confidante'."

You don't need to go on a Reality TV show or blast everything on Facebook. God already knows what your prayer is.

HE wants to see your sincerity, your raw honesty and how "effective & fervent" you are…your persistence in *"praying without ceasing"* HE wants to see your faith and patience to wait on Him.

"Prayer" is mentioned 184 times in the Bible. (NKJV)

http://www.biblegateway.com/keyword/?version=NKJV&search=prayer&searchtype=all&language1=en&spanbegin=1&spanend=73&resultspp=250

A few scriptures include:

Psalm 54:2 - Hear my **prayer**, O God; Give ear to the words of my mouth.

Matthew 21:22 - And whatever things you ask **in prayer**, believing, you will receive."

Romans 12:12 - rejoicing in hope, patient in tribulation, continuing steadfastly in **prayer**;

Philippians 4:6 - Be anxious for nothing, but in everything by **prayer** and supplication, with thanksgiving, let your requests be made known to God;

Colossians 4:2 - Continue earnestly in **prayer**, being vigilant in it with thanksgiving;

1 Peter 4:7 - But the end of all things is at hand; therefore be serious and watchful in your **prayers.**

Another question I pondered regarding the practice of praying: **Why collective or group prayer?**

James 5:16 - …The effective, fervent **prayer** of a righteous man avails much. (Imagine the power of more than one righteous man?)

2 Corinthians 9:14 - and by **their prayer** for you, who long for you because of the exceeding grace of God in you.

1 Thessalonians 1:2 - We give thanks to God always for you all, making mention of you in **our prayers**,

As we all strive to deepen and enhance our prayer life, always keep this poem in mind:

Prayers Can't Be Answered Unless They Are Prayed

— Helen Steiner Rice

A life without purpose is barren indeed;

There can't be a harvest unless you plant seed.

There can't be attainment unless there's a goal;

A man's but a robot unless there's a soul.

If we send no ships out;

No ships will come in.

And unless there's a contest;

Nobody can win.

For games can't be won unless they are played,

and Prayers Can't Be Answered Unless They Are Prayed!

So whatever is wrong with your life today,

You'll find a solution if you kneel down and pray.

Not just for pleasure, enjoyment and health,

Not just for honors, prestige and wealth.

But pray for a purpose to make life worth living,

And pray for the joy of unselfish giving.

For great is your gladness and rich is your reward,

When you make your life's purpose the choice of the Lord.

21
Seeing the Unseen in 2014

This is my church's theme for this new year.
Our Assistant Minister delivered a thought-provoking sermon based on this theme titled, "Will You See The Unseen in 2014?" He mentioned that *Things are not always as they appear.*

As I reflect on it, I think how I/we often miss "Seeing the Unseen" on a daily basis:

DO YOU SEE…the maid who cleans up your hotel room?
DO YOU SEE…the cashier who has to ring up your basket of "deals" during the Black Friday Pre-Holiday Rush…who gave up their Thanksgiving Family Gathering?
DO YOU SEE…the janitorial staff that cleans your office or your church building?
Do YOU SEE…the mechanic changing the oil on your vehicle?
Do YOU SEE…the attendant taking your ticket as you enter to enjoy a concert?
DO YOU SEE…the receptionist at your doctor's office?
DO YOU SEE…the postal delivery person, making sure you have your mail, no matter what the weather?
DO YOU SEE…the person waiting on you at the restaurant, who lives off of your tips?
DO YOU SEE…the person delivering your pizza?
DO YOU SEE…the Crossing Guard at your child's school?
DO YOU SEE…people's birthdays or those asking for prayer on Facebook?
DO YOU SEE…the family in your rear-view mirror at the McDonald's Drive-Thru, counting quarters for the Dollar Menu?
DO YOU SEE…people who have a smile on their face, but pain in their eyes?
DO YOU SEE…the Greeter at Walmart?

DO YOU SEE…the person in the mobility cart at the grocery store?
DO YOU SEE…the baby waving "Hi!" to you?
DO YOU SEE…the person who kindly let you in their lane, as you muscled your car in without blinking?
DO YOU SEE…the guys at the car wash cleaning your vehicle?
DO YOU SEE…the employee at the fast-food restaurant drive-thru window?

Will you rise to the call to take notice, extend kindness and be a blessing to others?

Will you pay attention and…**SEE THE UNSEEN in 2014?**

22
Be "Good for Nothing"

Bro. Gerald Lee, minister, and former Executive Assistant to the President of Southwestern Christian College, in Terrell, TX, was a guest minister at my church one Sunday several years ago. He preached a sermon that he called "Good For Nothing.".

He initially asked the audience, "How many of you feel that when people say to you, *'You ain't good for nothing,'* that it is a compliment?"

No one raised their hands. Many mumbled, "No." He explained that society has dubbed this to be a bad insult.

Our goal as Christians is to focus on "doing good" without expecting anything in return. By your faith and your sacrifice, God will reward you greatly.

Luke 6:34-36 (NKJV) says: *"And if you lend to those from whom you hope to receive back, what credit is that to you? For even sinners lend to sinners to receive as much back. But love your enemies, do good, and lend, hoping for nothing in return; and your reward will be great, and you will be sons of the Most High. For He is kind to the unthankful and evil. Therefore be merciful, just as your Father also is merciful."*

I am also reminded of an affirmation by John Wesley titled, **"All You Can."**

ALL YOU CAN
Do all the Good you can.
By all the Means you can,
In all the Ways you can,
In all the Places you can,
At all the Times you can,
To all the People you can,
As Long As Ever You Can.

Powerful Quotes to Remember:
"Never Get Tired of Doing Little Things for Others; Sometimes those Little Things Occupy the Biggest Part of their Hearts." – unknown

"We can't Help Everyone but Everyone can help Someone." – Ronald Reagan

"Be the Reason Someone Smiles Today." – unknown

"To the World you may be but one, but to One you may be the World." - unknown

"You have Never really lived until you have done something for someone who can never Repay You." – unknown

He asked the audience again,

"Now…Who wants to be known as **Good for Nothing**?"
(Everyone raised their hands and cheerfully stated "I do!")

Don't You??

23
"Are Ya' Feeling Me???"

(In Loving Memory of Sis. Pearl Steward, 98 years old, Laid to Rest 3/5/2014, R.I.P., Sweet Lady...)

I loved when this wonderfully-stern, yet hilarious woman would say this after explaining something to someone.

This was her way of asking, "Do you understand me?"

As human beings, we all thrive on the need to be understood.

Per Oprah Winfrey:

"I've talked to nearly 30,000 people on this show, and all 30,000 had one thing in common: They all wanted validation. If I could reach through this television and sit on your sofa or sit on a stool in your kitchen right now, I would tell you that every single person you will ever meet shares that common desire. They want to know: **'Do you see me? Do you hear me? Does what I say mean anything to you?'** http://www.oprah.com/oprahshow/The-Oprah-Winfrey-Show-Finale_1/7#ixzz2uZboPM9D

Validation is such a powerful quality. I know personally, it is an exhilarating feeling to feel that I am seen, heard and acknowledged.

I am reminded of a powerful moment on the mission trip I went on with the Schrader Lane Church of Christ in Nigeria, West Africa back in 1997. We were there to visit the Nigerian Christian Institute we help build and support. When we arrived, the entire campus, approximately 500 youth, were there to greet us. They looked at us with awe and wonder, as if we were celebrities, saying "The Americans are here."

I remember being overwhelmed by the attention, the excitement and a sea of blue uniforms.

After our Official Welcome by the headmaster, we headed toward our dormitory. Out of the habit of being a "Southern Girl" and "my Daddy's child," I smiled, squeezed the shoulder of one of the students, and said, *"Hi. How are you?"*

The response was amazing! It was like seeing a flower bloom in front of you! Her eyes lit up, she bowed and she replied, with the widest smile, *"Hello, Madame!"*

I whispered to the others in our group, *"We are not leaving until we have greeted every child here."* As the others did the same, it was like witnessing a valley of flowers blossoming at once. By the time we made it to the dormitory an hour later, I was an emotional mess. The children seemed to radiate profound gratitude that **"The Americans saw ME."**

From this day on, I will fondly ask others, whether verbally or mentally, after I explain something…especially something I am passionate about, as an homage to Sis. Pearl:

"Are Ya' Feeling Me???" ☺

24
"To Everything There Is A Season…"

Some of my favorite scriptures in the Bible are **Ecclesiastes 3:1-8 (NKJV)**. It describes how "Everything Has Its Time."

"**1 To everything there is a season, A time for every purpose under heaven:** 2 A time to be born, And a time to die; A time to plant, And a time to pluck what is planted; 3 A time to kill, And a time to heal; A time to break down, And a time to build up; 4 A time to weep, And a time to laugh; A time to mourn, And a time to dance; 5 A time to cast away stones, And a time to gather stones; A time to embrace, And a time to refrain from embracing; 6 A time to gain, And a time to lose; A time to keep, And a time to throw away; 7 A time to tear, And a time to sew; A time to keep silence, And a time to speak; 8 A time to love, And a time to hate; A time of war, And a time of peace."

http://www.biblegateway.com/passage/?search=Ecclesiastes%203&version=NKJV

Oftentimes, we are catapulted into a new direction, sometimes, against our will. Your life can instantly and unexpectedly take on a different trajectory than what you had planned or even imagined.

My new journey into blogging and writing is one that I had allowed LIFE to cause me to ignore. However, due to being awakened by unexpected health challenges, it has nudged me, excited me, amazed me, scared me and opened these "meteorological" emotions for me.

I am…

…**a volcano**, about to erupt lava, spewing inspiration, hope and love.

…**a hurricane**, hovering with intensity, refusing to move on.

…**a tsunami**, overwhelming me with a sense of purpose.

....**a tornado**, an awesome force of wind and debris of positive energy.

...**the sunlight**, blinding me with its radiance.

...**the wind**, nudging me forward.

....**the hail**, plummeting down and piercing me with inspiration.

....**the snow**, white flakes blinding me and exciting me about possibilities.

...**the fog**, to limit my visibility of negative people, thoughts and words.

....**the rain**, showering soft drops of refreshing ideas.

I am now like the Seasons...

...**the harsh, cold Winter**, to "freeze off" old doubts and fears.

...**the shift from Winter-to-Spring**, the renewing of my mind.

...**the vibrant Spring**, with colorful ideas, optimism and creativity.

...**the hot Summer**, burning away negative influences.

...**the crisp Fall**, ever-changing and revealing uncharted territory.

As it says: *"To everything there is a season, A time for every purpose under heaven."* It appears to be so for all of us.

Your "Season" is here...right now.

Be Still...Breathe...Look Up...and Pay Attention...

25
Going Through Your Stuff...

I recall when my grandmother passed away. My mother, her sisters, and the granddaughters had the ominous task of sorting through her things.

I was humbled by what I saw. Her Sunday suits and wide selection of hats were stored neatly in her closet. Her recipes were found hidden at the bottom of her cooking utensil drawer. She had new robes and gowns that were never worn. There were the "good towels" and "good dishes" that had never been used. These were to be saved for guests or "someone important."

Guess what? ***You are Important.***

I recall us sorting through her many albums of photos. The photos that no one knew who was in them or didn't want were simply thrown away. I am a photo "addict," having several boxes and many albums of photos from the past. I quietly asked my sister, *"Uhm...if I passed away, what would happen to my photo collection?"* She firmly stated, *"We'd probably keep some that you are in and trash the rest."* I gasped! She said, *"Why would we keep them? We don't know those people! These moments that you captured don't really mean anything to anyone but you."*

I learned several lessons from this experience:

- Don't get all obsessed with material things. You cannot take it with you.
- Instead of focusing on leaving "stuff" that will eventually be of no use, focus on leaving behind kindness, smiles and good deeds. These will remain forever.
- Be thankful and enjoy what you have...not about what you don't have.

Look around your home right now. If you died this very moment…what would happen to your "stuff?" Does it really matter???

Matthew 6:19-21(NKJV) says: *"19 Do not lay up for yourselves treasures on earth, where moth and rust destroy and where thieves break in and steal; 20 but lay up for yourselves treasures in heaven, where neither moth nor rust destroys and where thieves do not break in and steal. 21 For where your treasure is, there your heart will be also."*

My personal goal: One day, when I die, I hope to have left a "warehouse full" of encouragement, LOL moments, kindness, blessings and good-will that live on for generations to come. When people have to sort through my material possessions, I want everything to have been enjoyed and used…at least once.

Are you prepared to have someone "go through your stuff?"

Because, one day, they will…

26
My "Way of Thinking"

I have a friend who finds it difficult adhering to wise counsel, mentoring or good advice. Although he will hear you out, he will counter with, *"I can see what you are saying, but my way of thinking is…"* He would actually negate or erase everything you just said.

I began to analyze myself to see how I, in my own unique way, have actually done the same thing in my life.

We do this often because of fear, procrastination, excuses, insecurities or limited vision. However, a lot of this can be attributed to our lack of faith and disobedience to GOD.

I envision using my "way of thinking" with the Lord and quietly hearing him gently reply:

Me to the Lord: "If people would treat me better, then I would be more loving…"

The Lord: "If you were more loving, people would treat you better…"

"If I had more money, I would give more and handle it better…"

"If you gave more and handled it better, you would have more money…"

"If I could see some results, I would work out more…"

"If you would work out more, you would see some results…"

"If people were friendlier, I wouldn't be so unapproachable…"

"If you weren't so unapproachable, people would be friendlier…"

"The world would be more kind and loving, if people would change…"

"If people changed, the world would be more kind and loving…"

"If people feared God and were more faithful, they would stop all of this immorality…"

"People would stop all of this immorality, if they feared God and were more faithful."

"If people could learn to respect each other's differences, we would get along better…"

"People would get along better, if they could learn to respect each other's differences…"

"If people followed THE GOLDEN RULE, we would be kinder to each other…"

"We would be kinder to each other, if people followed THE GOLDEN RULE…"

Sometimes, we believe we are wiser than God. He states in **Isaiah 55:8-10** (NKJV): *'For My thoughts are not your thoughts, Nor are your ways My ways,' says the Lord. 'For as the heavens are higher than the earth, So are My ways higher than your ways, And My thoughts than your thoughts.'*

We might want to release our own "way of thinking" and embrace obedience to God…

27
Not About ME...

I got body-slammed with the harshness of this reality.

I found out that someone "whom I considered" a very dear friend had passed away. I was utterly devastated.

Primarily because:

I found out she had waged a 4-year battle with Pancreatic Cancer.

I had always included her in my Greeting Card Ministry, sending her Christmas cards & birthday cards (her birthday was a day after my Mom's)

I had considered her a very dear friend...
YET...she never let **ME** know...
I immediately went into my "Sentimental" mode:

- I reached out to a former work colleague. I had left the company over 17 years ago. He told me sadly, but with certainty: "Yes, she has passed away. She came by here about 4 months ago to tell us all good-bye."
- I found her home phone number and called. I spoke with her daughter, whom I recall her speaking so fondly of along with her son and husband. I told her that she probably didn't remember me but that I used to work with her mother and I adored her. I told her I was heartbroken that I didn't get to tell her how much I loved her and how much she meant to **me**. She quietly responded, "Ms. Janette, she knew."
- I wrote a heartfelt sympathy card to the family.
- I posted my condolences on Facebook.

I was in utter grief...

However, the day of the funeral, my MS kicked in high-gear. I was so physically-challenged that I could barely move…better yet drive.

I wept…because I knew that I could not go to the funeral.

My grief deepened…

FINALLY…the "Ah-Ha Moment" appeared…

I was making this ALL ABOUT ME…

- I initially said to myself, *"How could she have this cancer for 4 years and not tell* **ME***?"* For the first 2 years…I was out-of-state. Year 3 – I was trying to find out my own health mystery, as well as relocating back with **my** job. Year 4 – I had gotten **my** MS diagnosis, been laid off my job, and was experiencing denial and depression.
- I was so consumed with **ME** that I honestly was not thinking about anyone else or what they may be going through.
- I NOW realize that she was navigating her OWN storm and had done exactly what I did—only involving close family and friends..
- I was devastated that she did not share her storm with **me**…yet I never reached out to share my storm with her.
- I saw photos of her during her journey. I wept…thinking that I could have comforted her and helped her. I honestly felt that maybe I could have saved her.

Oh, so much about ME…

I now realize how I may have been received by her family…if I made it to the funeral, primarily to fulfill, what I perceived as, everyone else's expectation. I would have looked into the casket at "someone I once knew." I would have been greeted by her family as a stranger. They may have even wondered, "Where were **you** during the struggle?"

The reality is that I tend to make so many people who have passed through my life a PRIORITY when all I am to them is an OPTION. And the even harsher reality is that my actions or lack-there-of said the same to them...

Lessons Learned:

- **IT'S NOT ABOUT ME**... (look at all of the "I's" and "Me's" used in this reflection)
- Don't expect anything from anyone that you don't give yourself.
- You are not the center of everyone's universe, nor or they the center of yours. Only God is...or should be,
- Do the very best you can do. (Not what you think others expect you to do.)

I was shocked at the realization that, although I was hanging onto our close friendship 17 years ago, it was what it was. Neither of us had actively worked at staying connected...and no...my card ministry doesn't count. Both of our lives had drifted in different directions.

Although I had put our friendship up in my mind to be similar to one such as Oprah Winfrey and Gayle King's, in reality, it was not. We didn't talk every day nor were involved in each other's lives.

I am finally at peace with the love I feel for her and the precious time the Lord allowed for our paths to cross...

Rest In Peace, Dear One. Thank You for the Love We Shared...

28
"Cut Off Your Nose to Spite Your Face…"

I recall as a child, and even a young adult, wondering exactly what that phrase meant. It sounded interesting. I would actually stand in a mirror to try to visualize what this would look like.

Wikipedia explains this phrase: *"Cutting off the nose to spite the face" is an expression used to describe a needlessly self-destructive over-reaction to a problem: "Don't cut off your nose to spite your face" is a warning against acting out of pique, or against pursuing revenge in a way that would damage oneself more than the object of one's anger.*
http://en.wikipedia.org/wiki/Cutting_off_the_nose_to_spite_the_face

It further explains: *The expression has since become a blanket term for (often unwise) self-destructive actions motivated purely by anger or desire for revenge. For example, if a man was angered by his wife, he might burn down their house to punish her; however, burning down her house would also mean burning down his, along with all their combustible personal possessions.*

Our lawmakers appear to be quite ironic in their rationale regarding what makes sense for our country. The people they won't increase the minimum wage for are the ones they expect to serve their food; babysit their children; clean their houses; cut their lawns; wash their cars or anything making their lives convenient.

These are the same people they will affect by their desire to repeal the Affordable Healthcare Act. However, if you succeed, the people who desperately need healthcare and don't have access to it are the ones you rely on.

You think you are hurting me by cutting me off; but you are actually cutting yourself out of resources and encouragement.

People "hate" President Obama, but enjoy having healthcare, a recovered economy and automotive jobs. They are beneficiaries of his humility, kindness and diplomacy respected throughout the world.

I actually heard of a story of a White woman in need of public assistance. The ONLY person qualified to help her was an African-American woman. The woman in need resisted getting help simply because of her. She initially chose to "suffer" than to get available assistance. She grudgingly accepted...

Corporations that insist on spraying plants with pesticides and pumping animals with antibiotics for rapid growth and profits are eventually poisoning themselves and their future legacies.

"Only when the last tree has died and the last river has been poisoned and the last fish has been caught, we will realize that we can't eat money." — Cree Indian Proverb

The Bible notes this. Proverbs 30:33 (NKJV):*"33 For as the churning of milk produces butter, And wringing the nose produces blood, So the forcing of wrath produces strife."* The Lord is actually warning us to not provoke others to anger or we will suffer the consequences.
http://www.bibleabookoftruth.com/misquotedbiblequotes.pdf

People should realize...the boat you are poking holes in is the one you are riding in. You may drown the Captain, but you will also drown yourself...

29
Do You Really Want It?

There is a story of a young man telling an accomplished pianist:

"I want to be a famous pianist like you and perform at Carnegie Hall." The pianist replied, *"No you don't."* The young man persists, *"Of course I do. Why would you say that?"* The pianist calmly replies: *"Are you willing to practice 7- 8 hours a day, 7 days a week, healthy or sick? Are you willing to forego vacations, holidays, relationships and family? Are you willing to sacrifice EVERYTHING you know and love?"* The young man shook his head in regret and walked away. The pianist looked at him and sadly replied, *"I didn't think so…"*

We are all, at some point in our lives, guilty of this notion.

We SAY…**we want to lose weight**. Yet, our eating habits do not reflect a healthy diet.

We SAY…**we want to be debt-free**. Yet, our spending habits and lack of fiscal discipline are not reflective of this.

We SAY…**we want to get in shape**. Yet, our refusal to exercise and avoidance of the gym paint a different picture.

We SAY…**we want to be married**. Yet, our disdain for men, lack of communication skills and unwillingness to compromise do not equate to this outcome.

We SAY…**we want to be more knowledgeable & well-read**. Yet, our lack of study or reading will not result in this.

Our lives are often lived in conflict and contradiction. We DO what we say we don't want; and DON'T DO what we say we want. Example: We eat pizza when we say we want to be healthier. We don't do what the doctor recommends when it comes to feeling well.

We are often faced with this conflict spiritually. We SAY we want to go to Heaven, yet we struggle with our obedience to God and releasing the ways of the world.

The Bible mentions this:

Matthew 6:24(NKJV): "No one can serve two masters; for either he will hate the one and love the other, or else he will be loyal to the one and despise the other. You cannot serve God and mammon (riches)."

Romans 12:2 (NKJV): "And do not be conformed to this world, but be transformed by the renewing of your mind, that you may prove what is that good and acceptable and perfect will of God."

Revelation 3:15-17 (NKJV): "I know your works, that you are neither cold nor hot. I could wish you were cold or hot. 16 So then, because you are lukewarm, and neither cold nor hot, I will vomit you out of My mouth. 17 Because you say, 'I am rich, have become wealthy, and have need of nothing'—and do not know that you are wretched, miserable, poor, blind, and naked—"

Powerful Quotes to consider:

"The question isn't 'Can You?' It is 'Will You?'" – unknown

"Don't be upset by the results you didn't get with the work you didn't do." – unknown

"Turn Intentions into Actions." – unknown

"If you did what you always did, you will get what you always got." – unknown

"If nothing changes, nothing changes." - *unknown*

"You could make a wish or you could make it happen." - unknown

The question remains: ***Do You REALLY Want It?***

30
Down off the Pedestal

Recently, I was giving advice to a dear friend in the midst of some relationship challenges. I shared with him the "female perspective." I told him that when we women are in love, we can tend to do some irrational things. We can and will say and do some things that may be considered dumb, crazy and foolish. We make mistakes.

I was shocked when he replied, with honesty and sincerity, *"But not you, Sister Janette. Why, I have always thought that you were a perfect Christian. You never sin or make mistakes."*

I humbly said, *"Sweetie…that is far from the truth. I am going to need you to pull me off that pedestal. I am flawed. I ask the Lord DAILY for forgiveness of my sins in my thoughts, words and actions. I have, do and will make mistakes. I am imperfection personified. If you were to look up 'imperfect' in the dictionary, I would guess that my picture would appear!"* ☺

What does it mean to put someone **"up on a pedestal"**? A response on *Yahoo! Answers* revealed the following:

Mjolnir06 answered: *This is an English saying that normally refers to "glorifying or idealizing" an individual or individuals. To "place" or put someone "up on" a pedestal means to have high expectations about how they should behave. It's not just with people in highly visible positions of responsibility (world leaders, famous stars, etc.), we also do it with our friends and family, and especially partners in a relationship.*

Usually the problem of putting someone up on a pedestal has little to do with who they are or what position they hold, but more commonly our expectations of someone put them there. When they don't live up to our expectations, we lose our respect for them. Sometimes people do put themselves up on a pedestal by condemning others. But being human is part of life and even if we want to hold people to their claims of sainthood, they may disappoint us.

What is it that is disappointing to us? Is it disappointing because somehow it feels like they have lied to us? Yet, it should come as no surprise to us that all human beings are still human beings. But when someone doesn't live up to our expectations is it truthful to say that they are lying to us, or is it our expectations that are lying to us?

https://answers.yahoo.com/question/index?qid=20081030174547AAoxiqb

Often people put you up on a pedestal. Their thoughts are often revealed in language such as:

"You think you are better than…"

"You act like you think you are better than…"

"Well, not everyone has it all together like you have…"

"You are all 'Holier than Thou'…"

Unfortunately, we can slowly lift ourselves up on pedestals by being so judgmental of others.

I have to confess, I never thought I was perfect, but I boldly thought I had it all together and was in complete control of the direction of my life. I called myself a "Health Fanatic." When others would tell me how awesome, skilled, intelligent, professional and compassionate I was, I allowed my ego to run amuck and myself to be gently raised up on a pedestal.

However, after receiving the unexpected, devastating health diagnosis of MS and getting laid off of my job, all I could do was remember this nursery rhyme:

"Humpty Dumpty sat on a wall,

Humpty Dumpty had a great fall.

All the king's horses and all the king's men

Couldn't put Humpty together again."

http://en.wikipedia.org/wiki/Humpty_Dumpty

I felt shattered, broken, unrepairable, unlovable, "damaged goods" and insignificant. The drop from my "proverbial pedestal" was a long, scary and painful one.

Lessons Learned:

- Don't allow others to put you on a pedestal.
- The only one who ever walked this earth who was "perfect and sin-free" was Jesus Christ.
- The higher you are lifted on that pedestal, the longer the drop.
- The fall off the pedestal is very painful.
- Oftentimes, the ones lifting you up on the pedestal will be the ones celebrating your fall.
- Since no one is perfect, it can be very lonely up there, uplifted as someone you are not.
- The only one who should be *put on a pedestal*, revered and obeyed is THE LORD.

"What people think about me is none of my business." – unknown
"What God thinks about me is everything."

"We must shift focus from pleasing Man to pleasing God."

If someone has "put you on a pedestal" of perfection...*step down off of it IMMEDIATELY...*

31
You Have Been DISMISSED…

Dismiss is defined as *"to decide not to think about or consider (something or someone); to send (someone) away; to cause or allow (someone) to leave: to officially make (someone) leave a job; to end the employment or service of (someone)* http://www.merriam-webster.com/dictionary/dismiss

I had someone who I prioritized as a "dear friend" just disappear from my life. No explanation or warning. One day, I am pushing through my own health challenges to take many hours to proofread a very important assignment due in her graduate program…and next, nothing. I called and texted, initially out of concern. This is someone who had checked on me at least three times a day for months, since my health diagnosis. Now…nothing. I finally received a text saying, "I am very busy. It's time for Me to look out for Me!" She announced on Facebook that she was unavailable for the next two weeks. No contact from her whatsoever. Yet, during this time-frame, she has posted about attending receptions, barbecues, coffee dates and events with others.

WOW…it finally hit me…she no longer had time for ME.
I had been "dismissed."

I know me… I initially want to fix it…ask for forgiveness for any infraction I may have unintentionally committed. I naturally assume it is my fault. Yet the reality is…sometimes people will walk out of your life, no matter how loving you are to them…just because…

I have to constantly repeat **Proverbs 3:5-6 (NKJV)**: *"5Trust in the Lord with all your heart,* **And lean not on your own understanding***; 6 In all your ways acknowledge Him, And He shall direct your paths."*

Although I am one who always wants an explanation and for things to make sense, I have to surrender to the reality that it probably is not going to happen. I just have to TRUST GOD and keep moving forward...battered and bruised, but wiser...

Helpful Quotes:

"This is what I learned in all these years on this earth...If somebody wants to walk out of your life, let them go." — Tyler Perry's character "Madea"

"God often removes someone from your life for a reason. Think before you chase after them." - unknown

"When someone walks out of your life, let them. There's no use in wasting your time on people that leave you. What you make of yourself and your future is no longer tied to them. You may miss them. But remember that you weren't the one that gave up." - unknown

"Sometimes you have to let people go because they are toxic to you. Let them go because they take and take and leave you empty. Let them go because in the ocean of life when all you're trying to do is stay afloat they are the anchor that's drowning you." - unknown

I sadly remember the aching lyrics from the song by Bonnie Raitt:

"I can't make you love me; If you don't.

You can't make your heart feel Something it won't."

http://www.azlyrics.com/lyrics/bonnieraitt/icantmakeyouloveme.html

I have to accept it...I have been dismissed...and I have to learn to be O.K. with that...
(lowers her head...wipes her tears...grabs her cane...limps off into the sunset...)

32
Rising to Your Expectations

I have been a longtime believer in the concept that people will "rise to the expectations" you give them. This is most notable in children. If you keep telling a child that "You are bad!" they will become that. If you tell them, "You are amazing!" they will become that.

Cases in Point:

#1 - While watching Oprah Winfrey interview the late Dr. Maya Angelou, she recounted her troubled childhood. She said that one day her mother stopped on the street, looked her firmly in the eyes and said, *"I think you are one of the greatest women I have ever met. Mary McLeod Bethune, Eleanor Roosevelt and my mother…in that category."* Maya was stunned! She said, from that moment on, she thought to herself, *"Suppose she is right? I may have something of value, maybe not just to me…"* The rest is history…

http://www.oprah.com/own-master-class/Dr-Maya-Angelou-on-the-Power-of-Words-Video

#2 - I clearly recall being in Kindergarten, approximately 6 years old. The teacher asked the class, "What do you want to be when you grow up?" Of course, most students gave the typical childlike answers…"A Policeman…A Fireman…An Indian Chief." When she got to me, I replied, *"I don't really know…"* She knew I was a very bright student. She inquired further, "Why do you say that?"

I shrugged my shoulders and replied, *"Mommy and Daddy say that we (my triplet sisters and me) are going to be in the Top 10 of our High School Senior Class and that we are going to complete college. I don't know what any of that means. But that is what Mommy and Daddy say…"*

I never felt arrogant about it. It was just an ingrained expectation, as sure as daily teeth-brushing and bathing,

Guess What? We ranked #6, #7, and #8 in our High School Senior Class, and we all have earned Bachelors and Masters Degrees from college!

#3 - Several years ago, I volunteered as a Teacher with my church's summer education program. I was going to teach for a week. As the children filed into my classroom, there was one kid, we'll call him "Little Johnny Doe" that I immediately knew was going to be a challenge. He came in late, was disruptive, a class "clown", spoke rudely and made it quite clear that he did not want to be here. I quietly breathed and prayed as to how to handle him, yet make the class effective for all of the kids. Then, an idea emerged!

I had all of the kids tell me their name and give me a brief introduction.

As expected, Johnny was loud, rude and a jokester when doing his. He continued to be a distraction and disrespectful during the entire class.

As I was about to dismiss the class for the day, I smiled and said,

"Before we leave I would like to recognize someone." All of the kids looked at each other, somewhat confused.

I continued, *"I just want to give a huge Shout Out and Thanks to "Johnny Doe."* The other students looked at me in amazement…including "Little Johnny."

"Johnny, you are always on time; very respectful; attentive; and interested in the class. You are a great role model for the entire class. I am so proud of you and grateful to have you in this class. Thanks everyone. I will see you all tomorrow."

The other kids looked at me as if I had grown horns out of my head! "Little Johnny" had his mouth open, eyes wide, and looked at me certain that I must be on drugs! ☺ I looked at him deeply in his eyes to let him know that I was saying this with deep belief, conviction and pride. He walked out of the room…utterly stunned!

I repeated this mantra every day. "Little Johnny" was in shock. His expression seemed to say, "Are you seriously talking about me?" The other students unconsciously started looking to him to be what I was praising him for.

Guess What? After a few days, "Little Johnny" came to my class ON TIME. He was respectful, helpful, engaged and quiet! He not only emerged as the class "role model" I had told him he was, but he also set the bar of excellence that unconsciously encouraged the other students to do the same.

Other teachers came to me at the end of the program and said, "We don't know what you did, but our initial "problem child" has been awarded MOST IMPROVED, MOST HELPFUL and a Certificate of Leadership Excellence this summer. What in the world did you do??!!"

I reflected on it and calmly replied, "I encouraged him to rise to my expectations of him. And he did…" ☺

33
Settling for Mediocrity

I woke up at 3:05 a.m., abruptly and in disdain. Reality hit me hard. I quietly whispered to myself, "You are settling for mediocrity."

Mediocrity is defined as "the quality of something that is not very good; moderate ability or value." http://www.merriam-webster.com/dictionary/mediocrity

I realized that I needed to "raise my own expectations" for my life. Many of us are taught to set goals or have dreams.

Many of us do, but don't act on them. I realized that most of my adult life has been defined by my settling.

"A dream without a plan is just a wish." – unknown

Cases in Point:

High School: Instead of striving for #1, Valedictorian, I settled for #7.

College: Instead of pursuing my passion to be a Physician, I settled for an average GPA and a general Business Administration degree.

First Job: As a Sales Executive, and although I am naturally competitive, I settled for being one of the top quota-earning salespersons, instead of being Top Salesperson of the Year.

Church: Instead of being a vibrant, active, roll-your-sleeves-up servant, I have now allowed my current health challenges to have me settle as a beloved, "pew-occupying" member.

Health: Instead of rising up to be a "Thriver" and Overcomer, I am settling for "just managing."

Writing: Instead of New York Times Best-Selling Author, I am settling on hiding behind blogging and Facebook posts.

I MUST "raise my own expectations." This will unconsciously inspire other people to do the same.

I must see myself as I want to be – better yet, AS GOD SEES ME - not as I currently am. I must set the bar of where I want to be much higher than my mind can imagine. That's what faith in God is all about...

Even spiritually, our bars are raised too low. We should all strive daily:

Matthew 25:21 (NKJV): "His lord said to him, 'Well done, good and faithful servant; you were faithful over a few things, I will make you ruler over many things. Enter into the joy of your lord.' "

Hebrews 12:1-3 (NKJV): "...let us lay aside every weight, and the sin which so easily ensnares us, and let us run with endurance the race that is set before us, 2 looking unto Jesus, the author and finisher of our faith, who for the joy that was set before Him endured the cross, despising the shame, and has sat down at the right hand of the throne of God. 3 For consider Him who endured such hostility from sinners against Himself, lest you become weary and discouraged in your souls."

2 Timothy 4:6-8 (NKJV): "...I have fought the good fight, I have finished the race, I have kept the faith. 8 Finally, there is laid up for me the crown of righteousness, which the Lord, the righteous Judge, will give to me on that Day, and not to me only but also to all who have loved His appearing."

We SAY we want to go to Heaven...yet we are comfortable with our complacent, self-pleasing, All-About-Me existence here on Earth.

Are You Settling???

34
SPECTATOR of Our Own Lives

In my earlier years, I was somewhat of a "camera fanatic." I took pictures of everything. I felt so passionate about capturing every moment.

As I review my photos, I realize that in most events, my picture is not among them. I spent so much time capturing the moment that I failed to "live in, embrace or enjoy" the moment. I know I was there, but my photo albums don't reflect it.

We spend so much of our time watching 'Reality" TV and Entertainment shows. We read magazines and rely on Social Media sites like Facebook, Twitter and Instagram to inquire into others' lives. We do this in lieu of living our own.

Then, we realize that we have only been a "spectator" of our own life...and not a participant. So many of us "blow right past it." We rush through our entire day and our lives *unconsciously*.

Life is an accumulation of "NOW" moments. We often imagine life to be some big event or occurrence. It actually is the quilting together of simple, ordinary moments happening right now.

Most of us spend time comparing our lives to others or striving to live up to other people's definition of how we should live.

Powerful Quotes to Consider:
"Comparison is the thief of joy." – unknown
"Your time is limited so don't waste it living someone else's life. Don't be trapped by dogma – which is living with the results of other people's thinking." – unknown

"Don't compare your life to others. You have no idea what their journey is all about." – unknown
"Build your own dreams, or someone else will hire you to build theirs." – unknown.

God created us for a specific purpose. The Bible states in **Jeremiah 1:5 (NKJV):** "Before I formed you in the womb I knew you; Before you were born I sanctified you; I ordained you a prophet to the nations."

It would serve us all well if we "step down off of the bleachers and stop being spectators" in our own lives. Let's get in the game, have fun and enjoy our lives…

Shall We???

35
I Can't Want It More…

Most of us want the best for ourselves as well as others.

I have always had a personal commitment to want others to have opportunities and options.

I recall when I was planning to go on my first cruise and wanted a close friend to go with me. I even paid the initial deposit. When it was time to pay the balance, I was prepared to do that as well. However, her parents had decided that they were going to pay it. Nevertheless, she said she did not want to go. I tried every persuasive tactic that I could think of to convince her to go. She would say things like, "My parents can't afford it." I countered, "They are making an investment in you. They want you to see that the world is bigger than your small, hometown view." She still refused… It finally dawned on me…Her parents and I wanted it more for her than she did for herself…

The humbling lesson is that you cannot want anything for anyone more than they want it for themselves. Once you or someone makes a firm decision, help, resources and encouragement will overwhelm you. People will be "the wind beneath your wings;" the gasoline in your tank and enthusiastic cheerleaders to get you there. But…YOU HAVE GOT TO WANT IT FIRST.

One of my favorite lines in a movie was from *Rocky III*. It was Rocky and his wife Adrian on the beach. She forced him to admit he was afraid to fight Clubber Lane:

Adrian: "… *Apollo thinks you can do it, so do I. But you gotta want to do it for the right reasons. Not for the guilt over Mickey, not for the people, not for the title, not for money or me, but for you. Just you. Just you alone.* http://en.wikiquote.org/wiki/Rocky_III

Bonnie Raitt even mentions this in her 1991 hit song *I Can't Make You Love Me*. The song highlights that you cannot want a relationship more than the other person. The chorus says: *"I can't make you love me. If you don't. You can't make your heart feel Something it won't. Here in the dark In these final hours, I will lay down my heart And I'll feel the power; But you won't. No, you won't. 'Cuz I can't make you love me If you don't."* http://www.azlyrics.com/lyrics/bonnieraitt/icantmakeyouloveme.html

The Bible discusses this in **Matthew 10:14 (NKJV):** *"And whoever will not receive you nor hear your words, when you depart from that house or city, shake off the dust from your feet."* Jesus instructed his twelve disciples that, when they have tried to share the gospel with someone who doesn't want it for themselves, they must move on.

On the website www.4060men.com, an article titled "Wanting More for Someone Than They Want for Themselves," it says: *It is a matter of perspective, for sure, as you see something they apparently don't see. But the bottom line is that if you want something for somebody more than they want it for themselves, it is an unhealthy relational scenario. It reminds me of the quote I've written about some time ago that goes like this: "Any relationship is under the control of the person who cares the least." If you want an outcome for someone, even a good one, more than that person wants that outcome, you'll not only be frustrated in the relationship but also hurt in it. You got to let it go, really let it go, or your hurt and frustration will only damage the relationship.* http://www.4060men.com/read/blog/wanting-more-for-someone-than-they-want-for-themselves/

On the website Attitude Orange, this concept is discussed: "...I have seen the big possibilities in life. This positive outlook has prompted me to want to pass on to others my desire to excel. However, what is good for one person doesn't always apply to others. With time...I now realize that trying too hard for others helps no one if the other doesn't want it as well.

Also, what we may judge as being good for others may in fact not be good at all! Our perceptions are often colored by the sunglasses of our beliefs and our experiences and may lack the proper focus when it comes to the lives of others."

http://www.attitudeorange.com/en/do-you-want-more-for-others-than-they-do-for-themselves/

I can't want it more for you than you want it for yourself." – Janette McGowen

Bottom-line: *Time well-spent is in being the best YOU God and yourself want you to be. It is great to encourage, motivate and inspire others, but it has to be from where they are and want to go...not where you think they should go.* #LearningInProgress

36
My Favorite "INSULT"

One of the most amusing insults I have ever been given is:

"You think you are better than everyone..."

In the past I either dismissed this or went on the defensive by saying, "No, I don't…"

However, wisdom has taught me to remain silent and really listen to what is being said. I have learned to craft a clever, personal reply to this. It is:

"No…first of all…you don't know my thoughts because I have never shared them with you. So…this has to reflect YOUR thoughts about me. And for the record…I don't think I am better than anyone else. I may just want better for my life and am willing to work harder for it than most."

The Bible guides us:

Matthew 5:11 (NIV): "Blessed are you when people insult you, persecute you and falsely say all kinds of evil against you because of me."

1 Corinthians 15:33 (NIV): "Do not be misled: "Bad company corrupts good character."

Proverbs 13:20 (NIV): "Walk with the wise and become wise, for a companion of fools suffers harm."

Luke 6:27-28 (NIV): "…Love your enemies, do good to those who hate you, bless those who curse you, pray for those who mistreat you."

Romans 12:17-18 (NIV): "Do not repay anyone evil for evil. Be careful to do what is right in the eyes of everyone. If it is possible, as far as it depends on you, live at peace with everyone."

In an article titled "How to Determine Why Someone Is Treating You Poorly," more insight is given toward this:

Note how they act around you. Some of the possible signs might include: gossiping about you to others, ignoring you, saying hurtful things to you, breaking or stealing your stuff, belittling you, setting you up to get into trouble for something you didn't do or say, calling you names, implying that you're not as clever, good-looking, well-connected, valuable, etc. as them, intimidating you, leaving unfriendly/unkind messages about you on social networking sites, or breaking promises they swore they'd meet.

Ask yourself. Why do you need validation from them? Do you need them so much that you would have to supplicate them to make yourself better? It's fine if they don't like you, who cares? Remember you are being insecure and needy if you care.

Move on. Remember that there's no point in dwelling in the past. Get on with your life and activities, surround yourself by people who aren't mean to you, and focus on what matters to you.
http://www.wikihow.com/Determine-Why-Someone-Is-Treating-You-Poorly

Quotes to Consider:

"What you say about other people says a lot about YOU." – unknown

"Listen carefully to how a person speaks about other people to you. This is how they will speak about you to other people." – unknown

"People will always talk about you, especially when they envy you and the life you live. Let them. You affected their lives, they didn't affect yours." – unknown

"You talk a good game, but I'm watching how you play." – unknown

"Fact: Haters don't really hate you. In fact, they hate themselves because you are a reflection of what they wish to be." - unknown

However, one of the most profound words of wisdom for me is from Will Smith: **"Stop letting people who do so little for you control so much of your mind, feelings, and emotions."**

The thing that I do know with certainty is: I am a child of God. HE created me for a specific purpose. I will live my life in such a way that is pleasing to HIM, and strive every day to spend eternity with HIM.

37
Not Trying to Get Political…But….

In the realm of politics, I personally align with views from both political affiliations.

However, I tend to lean more toward one because: They at least RECOGNIZE and ACKNOWLEDGE my existence and the value of my VOTE.

ALL Political Parties…WAKE UP!

The USA no longer consists of WHITE-MEN-ONLY. It has become very diverse. Have you noticed?

- I would entertain your point-of-view if you had one. Just screaming "No!" to every piece of legislation proposed – with no proposal of what I can say "Yes" to…is quite disturbing and frustrating.
- You still haven't realized that MONEY cannot buy an election. How is it that you spent almost $1 billion dollars to defeat President Obama…and LOST? Based on the Constitution – that you so love bringing up – it grants each and every one of the US citizens (1) vote. Therefore, a Billionaire & a poor person – EACH have only (1) vote. You appear to be distracted by money and not votes.
(See 15th, 19th, and 26th Amendments.)
http://en.wikipedia.org/wiki/United_States_Constitution
- You exert all of your energy negatively and to the opposition. "What You Resist, Persists." – C.G. Jung. Mother Teresa once said, "I was once asked why I don't participate in ANTI-WAR demonstrations. I said that I will never do that, but as soon as you have a PRO-PEACE rally, I'll be there."

Instead of wasting time campaigning about what or whom you are AGAINST, why not try campaigning passionately about what YOU ARE FOR? *(This would definitely get my attention…and at least, earn my respect.)*

- Your candidate declares "47%" of Americans as ones whose VOTE does not matter. Thus, you ultimately got the results that you got.
- I am "sadly amused" when a political party yells "THEY just don't get it!" This brings me back to one of my favorite quotes: *"Sometimes, you are so passionate with preaching to others to GET OUT OF THE RAIN – that other people are staring at you – because you are the only one DRIPPING WET!"*
- You continue to make the mistake that people that don't agree with you are "Deaf and Blind."

We can HEAR your rhetoric…
We can SEE your actions…
People are fundamentally GOOD. We know basic right from wrong. WE believe in GOD and the Golden Rule. We can tell when this is authentic…and when it is a lie.

Politics has become a "scales of balance." You have to weigh the Pros vs. Cons of each side to determine which one more closely aligns with your own personal values and beliefs. You are not going to agree 100% with anyone.

I have personally held leadership roles in my past and can attest to the fact that it is virtually impossible to please even 10-20 people. Try pleasing 314 million…

ALL Political Parties would be wise to heed these humble words of advice, from a passionate, US citizen, who has her (1) vote…

AND I AM NOT AFRAID TO USE IT….

38
Judging vs. Good Judgment...

It is interesting how we totally misunderstand the difference between judging and good judgment.

Dictionary.com defines:

Judge:
Verb - to form a judgment or opinion of; decide upon critically; to decide or settle authoritatively; to infer, think, or hold as an opinion; conclude about or assess

Judgment:
Noun - the ability to judge, make a decision, or form an opinion objectively, authoritatively, and wisely, especially in matters affecting action; good sense; discretion

Matthew 7:1-5 (NKJV) talks about the mandate "Do Not Judge." It states: *1 "Judge not, that you be not judged. 2 For with what judgment you judge, you will be judged; and with the measure you use, it will be measured back to you. 3 And why do you look at the speck in your brother's eye, but do not consider the plank in your own eye? 4 Or how can you say to your brother, 'Let me remove the speck from your eye'; and look, a plank is in your own eye? 5 Hypocrite! First remove the plank from your own eye, and then you will see clearly to remove the speck from your brother's eye."*

Sometimes we get so busy judging others that we don't even notice that they are also judging you. Often, if we are not careful, we are worse than those we are judging. We often find people GUILTY and pass the sentence on what WE think it should be...when we had no authority to do so in the first place.

We should spend more time in using "good judgment" towards each other and making better decisions about our OWN lives.

NOW HEAR THIS: GOD did **not** appoint or anoint you as *"Judge of the Universe."*

HE already sees & knows everything we think, say or do…even before we think, say or do it.

As the younger generation says: **HE Got This!**

HE just needs you to be OBEDIENT, defined as "willing to do what someone tells you to do or follow a law."
 www.merriam-webster.com

God has lessons we all need to take. We need to STOP interfering with other people's lessons and TAKE YOUR OWN.

A harsh memory for me was when I was in the 3rd grade. I loved being a "Goodie-Goodie-Two-Shoes" and somewhat of a teacher's pet. Mrs. Limbaugh had told the class to stop talking or we would get a paddling. (I know…unheard of these days…but very effective.)

Well…I felt it was my DUTY to emphasize, loudly and with authority, this mandate to the class.

And guess what? Yep…she called me out into the hallway for a paddling! I couldn't believe it! I had broken the rule I was telling everyone not to!

My Mother was a Teacher's Assistant at the school. I was more petrified of her seeing me than I was of the paddling itself. Mrs. Limbaugh had pity on me. She had another teacher be on "look-out" for my mother, gave me 3 quick wacks of the paddle and allowed me to rush back into the classroom. Major lesson learned…

Reminds me of this profound quote:

"Sometimes, you are so passionate with preaching to others to GET OUT OF THE RAIN – that other people are staring at you – because you are the only one DRIPPING WET!"

39
Understanding the 23rd Psalm....

I clearly recall as a child learning the 23rd Psalm in Sunday School, as well as having it reinforced at home.

Psalm 23 (New King James Version)
23 The Lord is my shepherd;
I shall not want.
2 He makes me to lie down in green pastures;
He leads me beside the still waters.
3 He restores my soul;
He leads me in the paths of righteousness
For His name's sake.
4 Yea, though I walk through the valley of the shadow of death,
I will fear no evil;
For You are with me;
Your rod and Your staff, they comfort me.
5 You prepare a table before me in the presence of my enemies;
You anoint my head with oil;
My cup runs over.
6 Surely goodness and mercy shall follow me
All the days of my life;
And I will dwell in the house of the Lord
Forever.

I remember being confused by the first verse:
23 The Lord is my shepherd;
I shall not want.

I would scratch my head...confused...

"If the Lord is my Shepherd, why don't I want him?" ☺

The rest of the chapter seemed to indicate that he did great things for me. *Why would I not want him??*

A shepherd is defined as: "1. One who herds, guards, and tends sheep. 2. One who cares for and guides a group of people, as a minister or teacher." www.freedictionary.com

I took me awhile to understand that because HE is my Shepherd, I don't WANT for anything.

Awwwhhh….now it makes sense…I am relieved… ☺

40
"Are You Relevant in the 21st Century?"

The Question
I find myself in total amazement as I look at a calendar. We are rapidly approaching the second decade of the 21st Century.

This revelation reminds me of a multi-city career fair that I attended that was hosted by University of Phoenix and CareerBuilder called the "Re-Invent Your Future" Tour in Philadelphia, PA in August, 2010. The keynote speaker was Stedman Graham, New York Times best-selling author, educator and businessman, also well-known as the partner of Oprah Winfrey. He challenged the audience with a profound question:

"Are You Relevant in the 21st Century?"

What exactly does it mean to be "relevant?"
Webster defines relevant as *"having significant and demonstrable bearing on the matter at hand."* Synonyms are: Applicable, Pertinent, Relative, Material.
http://www.merriam-webster.com/dictionary/relevant

Let's consider these areas:
Are you Relevant?
...As a nation?
...As a company or organization?
...As an individual?

Are You Relevant...As a Nation?
We are The United States of America. We were the SUPER POWER, the absolute best of the best. "Made in America" was a signature of excellence. Our automobile industry was superior. Our education... untouchable.

The United States is currently ranked 14th in the world in education in STEM (Science, Technology, Engineering, Mathematics). http://www.guardian.co.uk/news/datablog/2010/dec/07/world-education-rankings-maths-science-reading

What went wrong? Why are we no longer #1? How did we lose our edge?

Are You Relevant ...as a Company or Organization?
2011 began a critical year for our country. This was the year that over 77.6 million people in the "Baby Boomer" Generation begin to retire. http://www.boomersweb.net/Baby-Boomers-Statistics.htm

As a company, are you ready?
- Do you have a succession plan in place?
- Have you been grooming individuals to replace them?
- Have you upgraded your systems and processes?
- Do you understand Cloud Technology? Are you utilizing Social Media?
- Have you gauged industry trends? Have you asked your customer base to see if your products and services are still useful to them?
- Are you in touch with your employees? Are they committed to your vision and mission – or are they looking to leave you?

Do you know?

Are You Relevant...as an Individual?
Many people have been traumatized by this economic crisis we are experiencing. Individuals who have worked in companies for 20 years have gotten laid off, and are now discovering that the skills they had at the former job are no longer RELEVANT.

They became top executives working their way up the corporate ladder with only a High School Diploma and hard work.

Yet, they are now being informed that, although they have a wealth of experience, a college degree and savvy computer skills are necessary.

- Have you evaluated your skills? Have you upgraded them?
- Do you have the education you need? Are you current with modern technology?
- Are you current with Social Media? – such as Facebook, LinkedIn, Twitter, Blackberry; IPhone; IPad; Skype, Kindle, Nook....
- Do you know the current economic and business trends?
- Do you read daily to stay informed?

Our economy is now Global. Are You??

Thus, the next, compelling question is:

What Can We Do?

As a Nation:
We have to take education as seriously as the rest of the world. Our archaic education system based on an Agriculture/Farming necessity is obsolete. We must have a major overhaul.

"The 21st century isn't coming; it's already here.... Public schools must prepare our young people to understand and address global issues, and educators must re-examine their teaching strategies and curriculum so that all students can thrive in this global and interdependent society."
http://thejournal.com/articles/2010/04/08/21st-century-skills- evidence-relevance-and-effectiveness.aspx

Students in the highest-ranking countries begin their formal education as young as 2 years old. They attend school 12-16 hours a day, oftentimes 6 days a week....YEAR ROUND.

We have to regain our level of excellence in what we make and produce to once again proclaim "Made in America" has value. We cannot even rest on the notion of being the 10th Happiest Country in the world.
http://www.forbes.com/2011/01/19/norway-denmark-finland-business-washington-world-happiest-countries.html

We must realign with the values that were proclaimed in the Declaration of Independence:

"We hold these truths to be self-evident, that all men are created equal, that they are endowed by their Creator with certain unalienable rights, that among these are life, liberty and the pursuit of happiness."
http://www.ushistory.org/DECLARATION/document/index.htm

As a Company or Organization:
We must start TODAY mentoring and training employees to back-fill the jobs of the rapidly- retiring, millions of Baby Boomers.

We must get back to the basics of asking our employees and our clients, "How are we doing? Are you satisfied with the products and services we are providing you?"

We must embrace and implement change, not only locally, but globally.

We have to gather, assimilate, and implement information faster. We have to embrace technology. With the power of the Internet, your business can expand beyond our borders to elevate you as a global player in the business arena.

And finally….

As an Individual:
You must "change the way you think" and learn how to process information more efficiently. You must do your own self-assessment or seek one professionally by a career counselor, mentor or coach. Go back to school to earn your education. With the enormous popularity of the convenience of ONLINE Education, you can do this in less time than many traditional schools. Learn modern technology – Texting, Smartphones and Social Media. READ MORE. Be informed by global news shows like CNN.

"The illiterate of the 21st Century will not be those who cannot read and write, but those who cannot learn, unlearn and relearn." – Alvin Toffler

At the end of the day…..we all have to ask ourselves the question…

Are You Relevant in the 21st Century??

Are You???

41
"Ain't Nobody Got Time For That!"

This phrase went "viral" on YouTube and the internet when a KFOR News Channel 4 Reporter asked a resident named Sweet Brown her account of escaping a fire that broke out at her apartment complex.

She said, "Well, I woke up to go get me a cold pop; then I thought somebody was barbecueing. I said, 'Oh, Lord Jesus, it's a fire!' Then I ran out...I didn't grab no shoes or nothing... Jesus...I ran for my life! And then the smoke got me. I've got bronchitis. ***Ain't Nobody Got Time For That!***"

http://www.youtube.com/watch?v=udS-OcNtSWo

This interview has been remixed as a music parody, and "Sweet Brown" has become an overnight celebrity. All of this due to her real-life brush with death.

Although, it was somewhat comical, none of us honestly know what we will say if asked to recount a life-threatening experience on-the-spot.

Regardless, I find myself using this phrase quite often now as I assess things in my life. Here are a few:

Dealing with major health challenges...

Sweating the Small Stuff...

Caring what people say about me...

Begging for people to forgive me...

Not forgiving others...

Taking Advice from people who don't know anything...

Expecting everyone I care about to care about me...

Worrying about what others think about me...

Not making GOD the #1 Priority in my life...

Not making MYSELF the #2 Priority in my life...

Not Being Happy...

Not Operating Healthier…

Doing what the World Does…

Being Afraid to say "No"…

Trying to be everything to everybody…

Not planning to fail but failing to plan…

Needing approval, praise or validation from others…

Being paralyzed by FEAR…

When confronted with life's complicated and conflicting challenges, just remember to utter the famous words of Sweet Brown:

"Ain't Nobody Got Time for That!" ☺

42
"Why Do We Do What We Do?"

Have you ever taken the time to ask yourself this question?

We drive the same way to work; comb our hair the same way; eat the same foods; watch the same news TV station; etc. Oftentimes, with no thought, rhyme-or-reason, or rationale as to why we did this..

Maybe it's out of Habit. Maybe it is Laziness. Maybe it is Complacency. Maybe, we are stuck in our Comfort Zones. Maybe it is Fear. Maybe it is out of Tradition.

If we would take the time to understand why we do what we do, we may discover an easier; cost-effective; happier; more satisfying way to enjoy our lives...

Reminds me of a story:
There was a young, newly-wed couple. The woman was attempting to cook her first Christmas Dinner.

Her husband watched proudly as she cautiously took a mouth-watering, tantalizing, juicy, large Country Ham out of the oven. She basted it with its wonderful juices and prepared to place it in a serving pan. She abruptly grabbed a large, carving knife and deliberately chopped off both ends! Two perfectly, edible sections of ham discarded.

Her husband was shocked! He asked her why she did this. She shrugged her shoulders and responded, **"That is the way my mother always cooked it."**

The husband was perplexed. He approached his new Mother-in-Law and asked her why she did this.

She responded, *"That is the way my mother always cooked it."*

Determined to get to the bottom of this mystery, he approached his new Grandmother.

He asked her why she did this. She responded,

"Because my serving pan was too small..." ☺

43
Will God Even RECOGNIZE You??

I am reminded of a joke:

A woman had just turned 40 years old. She asked the Lord, "How much longer do I have to live?" HE replied, "You should live for an additional 50 years."

She was so thrilled that she went and had a face-lift, liposuction, tummy tuck, got her hair cut and colored, got tattooed, lost 50 lbs., got new dental work...a Total Extreme Makeover.

As she was happily, crossing the street one day, she was struck by a distracted driver and killed.

As she was waiting to enter the Pearly Gates of Heaven, she asked, "God? I thought you said I had 50 more years to live?"

HE replied, "I know my child, but you looked so different, I didn't recognize you..." ☺

Although, this is a funny...it does call into question...

Will God Recognize You as "one of HIS own" on the Day of Judgment?

Do you think, speak and act so much like the world, that no one recognizes you as a Christian?

People love using the excuse: *"God knows my heart."* Actually...HE does.

HE said that our bodies are temples:
1 Corinthians 6:19-20 (NKJV): " *Or do you not know that your body is the temple of the Holy Spirit who is in you, whom you have from God, and you are not your own? For you were bought at a price; therefore glorify God in your body and in your spirit, which are God's.*"

We are also supposed to adhere to:

Romans 12:2 (NKJV): *"And do not be conformed to this world, but be transformed by the renewing of your mind, that you may prove what is that good and acceptable and perfect will of God."*

Satan is so cunning. He has us *"brain-washed"* to believe that we must **look like, be like, act like and talk like** the world or we are "uncool," "out-of-touch," "backward" and so "un-21st Century."

I don't know about you, but I am NOT here to impress the world.

Plus…people can be TRIFLING. The ones who love you today, are against you tomorrow.

This is why I am not a Beyonce' – Justin Bieber – Katy Perry – Taylor Swift – One Direction loyalist. Although I respect their talent, they are just human beings who are now on the national and international stage. *If their sole purpose isn't to help draw you closer to GOD, what is the point?*

Unfortunately, Satan has them convinced that their talent and popularity is all about THEM…not about our Creator, who blessed them with these gifts.

Don't you want to be like Jesus Christ?

I find myself challenged by this quote:

If you were on trial for being a CHRISTIAN, would there be enough evidence to find you GUILTY?

44
"What's in Your (Spiritual) Wallet?"

Most of us are familiar with the TV commercial for Capital One's Quick Silver credit cards. The spokesperson, TV actor Samuel L. Jackson asks, *"What's In Your Wallet?"*

Our credit cards are considered one of our most important purchasing tools we have with us. Most of us also have the following items in our wallets: Cash, Driver's License, Insurance Card, Membership Cards, Wallet Photos, Receipts...and yes, even Lottery Tickets.

This led me to ask what should be in my "spiritual wallet?"

The Bible tells us:

1 Corinthians 13:13 (NKJV): 13 And now abide faith, hope, love, these three; but the greatest of these is love.

Galatians 5:22-23 (NKJV): 22 But the fruit of the Spirit is love, joy, peace, longsuffering, kindness, goodness, faithfulness, 23 gentleness, self-control. Against such there is no law.

Thus, we should have:

Faith – Hope – Love – Peace – Patience (Longsuffering) – Kindness – Goodness – Faithfulness – Gentleness – Self-Control

Other items to include may be:

Gratitude – Joy – Contentment – Perseverance – Resilience

These qualities should take up residence in our minds, mouths, hearts and souls.

Since Satan is a cunning "thief," possession of these would be great Theft Protection and Identity-Theft Prevention deterrents.

The Capital One Quicksilver card helps you "Earn Unlimited 1.5% Cash Back on All purchases."

Just like the earthly credit card helps you earn "cash back rewards," God offers us an eternal reward with Him.

Luke 6:23 (NKJV): "Rejoice in that day and leap for joy! For indeed your **reward** is great in heaven, For in like manner their fathers did to the prophets."

Colossians 3:24 (NKJV): "knowing that from the Lord you will receive the **reward** of the inheritance; for you serve the Lord Christ."

It may be wise to evaluate what's in your "spiritual wallet" on this journey called "Life," as we all strive toward our reward from the Lord.

45
Blessing or Lesson?

As I was reviewing my resume, I was reflecting on work colleagues I had at each one of my previous jobs who made a positive impact on my career and my life.

Unfortunately, a few were not very favorable. Then I remembered the quote: *"Everyone who comes into your life is either a blessing or a lesson."* - unknown

It also gave me pause to realize that I ONLY remembered the names of those who made an impression in my life.

I remembered one former colleague specifically at one of the earliest jobs in my career. He and I were close. He "got me" and gave me optimism, acceptance and encouragement while we worked together. Our lives have moved in different directions. We have been out of touch for almost 20 years. However, I was curious to know how he was. I found him on LinkedIn. I wasn't sure he even remembered me. He was thrilled to reconnect! I was humbled that he remembered me so fondly. I was so privileged to be able to tell him how much I appreciated him.

I also remember those who mistreated me. Now that I am wiser, I can cut through the hurt feelings, the betrayal and devastation. I can clearly see the lesson in each of those situations. When people come into your life who are evil towards you, it's usually not about you. It is about them. Our first impulse is to seek revenge and karma. This will not work. The Lord has stated in **Romans 12:19 (NKJV):** *Beloved, do not avenge yourselves, but rather give place to wrath; for it is written, "Vengeance is Mine, I will repay," says the Lord.*

We may try to state our case on Judgment Day: "Lord, didn't you see what John Doe did to me!"

The Lord may respond: "Of course I did, my child. I see and hear everything. I will deal with John Doe when he has to face me. I am dealing with YOU right now. I want to know how YOU dealt with John Doe."

I am constantly humbled by these words: *"When someone mistreats you, without forgiveness, you become them."* – Dr. David Jones, Jr.

The challenge is to strive to live your life so that people who have crossed or will cross your path consider you a *blessing to savor* and not a *lesson to have learned*. It could be as deep as a friend, relative or work colleague or as casual as in an elevator, a waiting room or in a check-out line. It is my prayer that people will remember me and my name with a warm smile and fond memories of our encounter, regardless of how long or brief it may be.

As the years go by, you may not remember every person whose path you have crossed. The humbling thing is that they will remember you.

"People will forget what you said; People will forget what you did; but People will never forget how you made them feel." – Dr. Maya Angelou

Are You Someone's Blessing or Lesson?

46
Unsolicited Advice

Advice is defined as "an opinion or suggestion about what someone should do; recommendation regarding a decision or course of conduct." **Unsolicited** is defined as "not searched or asked for." http://www.merriam-webster.com

A dear friend of mine has adamantly insisted on her disdain of what she calls "unsolicited advice." Her definition is when others feel the need to give you advice that you neither asked for nor are they offering any resources to support, i.e. money, time, options, etc.

One of the things that I am working on, on my journey of spiritual and personal growth, is to no longer give unsolicited advice.

"We don't see things as they are, we see them as WE ARE."- Anais Nin

I realize that in my life, I have given people heart-felt advice, and was disappointed and stunned if they did not follow it.

As I grow in wisdom, I am more cognizant that I may have given advice based on my experiences and how I see the world, not how it really is.

I recall an instance while I was in college. I had went to my hometown and visited with my older brothers. They were making some choices that I personally did not think were very wise. One looked at the other and inquired, "Why don't you give us all the advice everyone else is giving us?" I calmly looked at them both and replied," Well…first of all, you guys are my big brothers. Shouldn't you be advising me? Secondly, if you are not going to follow Mom's advice (which I agree with), who am I? Finally, I can't swoop in and tell you how to live your lives and return to college to live mine. We all have one life to live."

Key phrases to be aware of are:

"If I were you, I would…"

"You ought to…"

"What you should do (say, or think) is…"

"What has always worked for me is…"

I had a recent experience where I was "advised" what to think, what to say, how I should express my faith, how I should handle my health challenges, how I should express myself in the written word as well as on Social Media, etc. In the past, I would spend passionate time expressing my point-of-view and countering this rationale. I would also doubt myself and try to adapt to someone else's opinion of my life.

Newfound wisdom is teaching me to "remain silent."

My relationship with God does not dictate an explanation to anyone. When you are being "led by HIM," you must cut out the chatter and focus ONLY on Him.

I must stay in close communion with Him. I have fallen in the past to adhering to advice from people who believed they knew me and knew the direction my life should go.

I have been told to be aware of the message I am giving and what I am trying to communicate. What people don't know is that the message is NOT COMING FROM ME. It is coming THROUGH ME. I HAVE to communicate it…I have no choice. For the first time in my life, I have to ignore this human "chatter," even masked under spiritual intent.

I don't know why I am writing and blogging or why I have become more open as I have about my life and my current health challenges. I personally have always been a very private person. Maybe God needs me to say this so that others can be led to Him? I really don't know.

I find that I am quoting like a mantra **Proverb 3:5-6 (NKJV)**: *"5 Trust in the Lord with all your heart, And* **lean not on your own understanding**; *6 In all your ways acknowledge Him, And He shall direct your paths."*

For once in my life, I am just going to surrender and see where God is leading me. I must....

So...Thanks, but No Thanks.

God's Advice and Direction is All I Need...

47
Trouble at the Gate

Many of us who travel on airplanes now understand the "drill" of going through the TSA Security Checkpoint. It goes something like this:

- Grab a bin
- Empty all of your belongings into it
- Remove your shoes and deposit into the bin
- Remove your jacket and place in the bin
- Put your laptop in the bin
- Place all jewelry, watches, coins, belts, metal objects, etc. into bin
- Place bin on the conveyor belt to be X-rayed by the Security Personnel.
- (In some airports, you walk through and get a body scan)
- If all is well: you walk through, gather your belongings and head to the gate.
- If not: You may have to go through it again; get "waned" down or possibly denied the ability to move forward.

Something for us all to consider is: **As we are approaching the "gate" entrance into Heaven, will we make it through?**

I recall a scenario I experienced at the TSA Security Checkpoint at the airport several years ago. My parents, sister and I had gotten special boarding passes so we could go to the gate to meet my nephew as he was arriving from his 2nd one-year army tour of duty in Iraq. As we were approaching the Security area, our strategy was that I would go through first, then my parents and then my sister. This way we would ensure that my parents made it through.

I breezed right through. My Mom was adamant that my Dad go through correctly. (Neither are frequent travelers, but she wanted to make sure he had no coins, pocket knives or belts on.) He made it through.

My Mom decided she was going through with a jacket on. Although we tried to tell her she couldn't, she was determined to do so anyway. "Ding-Ding," goes the warning. She went through again…had her sandals on. "Ding-Ding." The third time…"Ding-Ding." This time, we were perplexed. The TSA Agent asks, "Have you had any type of surgeries?" In unison, we say, "Knee Replacement." The agent led Mom to another area to swipe her with a security wane. My Dad and sister were putting their shoes back on and retrieving their belongings.

My nephew was exiting past us from the arrival gate in his military fatigues and saw us all in the Security area. (My Mom had proudly told the TSA Agent about her grandson's anticipated arrival.) When she saw him, she shouted with glee to the Agent, "There he is!" The agent and my Mom are hugging! His shocked face…priceless. ☺

Lessons Learned:
1). Before you worry about someone else getting through the gate, make sure you are doing what it takes to make it through yourself.
Matthew 7:1-5 (NKJV): *"Judge not, that you be not judged. For with what judgment you judge, you will be judged; and with the measure you use, it will be measured back to you. And why do you look at the speck in your brother's eye, but do not consider the plank in your own eye? Or how can you say to your brother, 'Let me remove the speck from your eye'; and look, a plank is in your own eye? Hypocrite! First remove the plank from your own eye, and then you will see clearly to remove the speck from your brother's eye. "*

2). Make sure that your OWN soul is prepared to meet the Lord.
Even on the plane, the flight attendant says, while giving you safety instructions, "In case of loss of cabin pressure, oxygen masks will automatically fall from the ceiling. If you are accompanied by children or others, PLACE YOUR MASK ON FIRST."
2 Peter 1:10 (NKJV): *"Therefore, brethren, be even more diligent to make your call and election sure, for if you do these things you will never stumble;"*
2 Timothy 2:15 (KJV): *"Study to shew thyself approved unto God, a workman that needeth not to be ashamed, rightly dividing the word of truth."*

3). God gives us free moral will. We can do whatever we want whenever we want. However, he does require our obedience. We can't have both.
Although we have free moral will and can do what we want to, if we are not obedient, we will find ourselves having *"gate trouble."*

Is your "call & election sure?"

Will You Make It Through the Gate?

48
"Thrown Under the Bus…"

We often hear warnings, especially in the workplace, about "being thrown under the bus." This basically means: being betrayed; being unsupported or being sacrificed for someone else's benefit.

To throw (someone) under the bus is an idiomatic phrase in American English meaning to sacrifice another person (often a friend or ally), who is usually not deserving of such treatment, out of malice or for personal gain. The phrase has been widely popularized by sports journalists since 2004 and was picked up by the mainstream media during the 2008 primary season. It has frequently been used to describe various politicians distancing themselves from unpopular or controversial figures. David Segal, a writer for The Washington Post, calls the expression "the cliché of the 2008 campaign."
http://en.wikipedia.org/wiki/Throw_under_the_bus

The phrase means utter betrayal or sudden brutal sacrifice of a loyal teammate for a temporary and often minor advantage.
http://www.examiner.com/article/what-is-meant-by-thrown-under-the-bus

An example of this was during the 2012 elections. Republican candidate Mitt Romney, during a heated debate with Incumbent President Barack Obama said he would eliminate PBS (Public Broadcasting Service), an American broadcast television network, as a means of reducing our national spending. Since one of the most popular, long-time, educational programming is *Sesame Street*, it was surmised that he was literally "throwing BIG BIRD under the bus" for his own benefit.

Sesame Street character Big Bird's name came up at Wednesday night's first presidential debate between President Obama and Mitt Romney. During the first presidential debate Wednesday night, GOP challenger Mitt Romney said he would cut funding for PBS, even though he is a fan of Big Bird.

As Romney noted what entities he would stop funding, he mentioned the president's health care law, then added that he would also stop a subsidy to PBS. He said to moderator Jim Lehrer, who works for PBS: **"I'm sorry, Jim. I'm going to the stop the subsidy to PBS. I'm going to stop other things. I like PBS. I love Big Bird. I actually like you, too. But I'm not going to keep on spending money on things to borrow money from China to pay for it."**

http://www.washingtonpost.com/politics/decision2012/big-bird-in-the-presidential-debate-mitt-romney-advocates-cutting-funding-for-sesame-street-pbs/2012/10/04/f7f280ba-0e1f-11e2-bb5e-492c0d30bff6_story.html

The Bible addresses this simply in **Matthew 7:12 (NKJV)**, or known as *The Golden Rule*: "Therefore, whatever you want men to do to you, do also to them, for this is the Law and the Prophets."

Two warnings that I personally came up with and live by include:

"If someone is trying to throw you under the bus, it would be wise if you'd stop running beside it." – Janette McGowen

"Be careful of throwing someone under the bus. Remember…it DOES shift into REVERSE."- Janette McGowen

Bottom-line: We all must be diligent in avoiding unhealthy conflict and preparing, in case it occurs.

In the wise advice of our elders: *"Prepare for the Worst. Hope for the Best."*

49
"Float like a Butterfly, Sting like a Bee…"

"Float like a Butterfly, Sting like a Bee. The hands can't hit what the eyes can't see."

"The Rope-a-Dope" – Ali's boxing strategy

"Rumble in the Jungle" – Ali vs. George Foreman, 1974

"Thrilla in Manila" – Ali vs. Joe Frazier, 1975

These phrases and events were/are synonymous to the legendary boxer Cassius Clay, aka **Muhammad Ali**. I grew up in awe of him as an amazing athlete and an international humanitarian.

His strong self-confidence was often mistaken as arrogance. However, he would say. ***"It ain't bragging – if you can back it up."***

He was a master of "psychological warfare." Without being a clinical psychologist, he would repeat to his opponent over and over "You are going down in the 3rd Round. You are going down in the 3rd Round." Guess what? He would knock them out in the 3rd Round!

Some of his "rants" of confidence included:

"If you even dream about beating me, You'd better wake up and apologize."

"I'm so mean, I make medicine sick."

"I'm young; I'm handsome; I'm fast; I'm pretty; and can't possibly be beaten."

"I'm so fast that last night I turned off the light in my hotel room and was in bed before the room was dark."

"I AM THE GREATEST. I said this even before I knew I was."

The stands he took were amazing. He competed and won Olympic Gold for USA in 1960, yet came home to still be treated with discrimination under Jim Crow Laws. When he refused to be drafted into the military during the Vietnam War, He said, *"Why am I going to fight people who have done nothing to me for a country that mistreats me."*

He had converted to Islam and sited religious beliefs as his reason for not going. His case made it all the way to the Supreme Court, where he was eventually vindicated.

His banter and on-going dialogue with ABC Sports Journalist Howard Cosell were epic! He challenged him to be a better reporter.

http://en.wikipedia.org/wiki/Muhammad_Ali

He definitely was considered "before his time."

However, I challenge that he was RIGHT ON TIME.

He will always be my most inspiring Athlete of all Time.

Muhammad Ali's quotes regarding life:

"I hated every minute of training. But I said, 'Don't Quit. Suffer now and live the rest of your life as a champion.'"

"It isn't the mountains ahead to climb that wear you down. It's the pebble in your shoe."

"Impossible is not a declaration, it's a DARE."

"Don't Count the Days, Make the Days Count."

"Age is whatever you think it is. You are as old as you think you are."

"God gave me this illness (Parkinson's Disease) to remind me that I am not Number One; He is."

"Service to others is the rent you pay for your room here on earth."

Probably, one of his most profound quotes that I admire:

"We have one life, it soon will be past;
What we do for God, is all that will last."

50
"EXERCISES" to Avoid and to Embrace

Society has bombarded us with the need to work out and exercise our physical bodies. However, we neglect exercising ourselves "spiritually."

Oftentimes, we get so exhausted by thinking, saying and doing things that do not serve us well. We often exert energy and resources that are of no benefit to ourselves, to others or to GOD.

Here are a few "Exercises" to AVOID:
JUMPING to conclusions
RUNNING our mouths
STRETCHING the truth
BENDING the rules and our backs for people who don't care
BREAKING our necks to be liked or to please others
STEPPING on others toes
STOMPING on others' feelings
KICKING someone when they are down
SITTING on the sidelines
BEATING yourself up with negative "self-talk" and for lack of perfection
THROWING unfair "punches" at others and yourself
SWEATING the small stuff
FALLING short of reaching your goals and quitting
SWIMMING in debt and despair
PUSHING aside signals our bodies give us
LIFTING WEIGHTS of guilt and resentment
SITTING on your excuses and best intentions
SKIPPING meals and important time with your children and loved ones

Our time, energy, peace-of-mind and resources may be better spent if we redirected our minds toward better options.

New *"Exercises"* to EMBRACE:

REACHING for the stars and our dreams
STEPPING out on faith
SQUASHING out lies and gossip
STANDING on the promises of GOD
WORKING OUT your soul salvation - *Revelations 20:13 (NKJV)*
TONING your words, emotions and attitude
LEANING on the "everlasting arms"
RUNNING "with endurance the race that is set before us"- *I Cor. 9:24 (NKJV)*
LIFTING your spirits and mood
SHAKING OFF criticism and negativity
CHANGING your attitude
BUILDING "your hopes on things eternal"
BOOSTING your energy toward serving others
SHARPENING your saw (by reading, studying God's word and constantly learning)
TRAINING yourself to be "swift to hear, slow to speak, slow to wrath" *James 1:10 (NKJV)*
EXERCISING discipline and commitment
INHALING clean air and peace
EXHALING stress, worry and fear
MEDITATING on the word of God (The Bible)

A Few Motivational Thoughts Include:

"Change the way you think and the way you think will change." – Wayne Dyer

"Don't be upset by the results you didn't get with the work you didn't do."

"Have your ever pushed yourself to your limit? Then how do you know that you have one?"

"It is never too late to become what you might have been." – George Eliot

"Life begins at the end of your Comfort Zone." - Neale Donald Walsch

"If you give up at the first sign of struggle, you really aren't ready to be successful." – Kevin Hart

"Don't expect to see a change if you don't make one."

"I can do all things through Christ who strengthens me.' – Philippians 4:13 (NKJV)

Let's all develop, embrace, and commit to an "enhanced" daily workout routine. In the mantra from Nike: *"Just Do It!"* ☺

51
"Because…I'm HAPPY!"

One of the most popular, international anthems is the Oscar-nominated song by Pharrell Williams from animated movie "Despicable Me 2" titled *Happy*. A few of the lyrics are:

It might seem crazy what I'm about to say

Sunshine she's here, you can take away

I'm a hot air balloon, I could go to space

With the air, like I don't care baby by the way

Because I'm happy

Clap along if you feel like a room without a roof

Because I'm happy

Clap along if you feel like happiness is the truth

Because I'm happy

Clap along if you know what happiness is to you

Because I'm happy

Clap along if you feel like that's what you wanna do

Here come bad news talking this and that

Yeah, give me all you got, don't hold back

Yeah, well I should probably warn you I'll be just fine

Yeah, no offense to you don't waste your time

Here's why

Because I'm happy…

http://www.metrolyrics.com/happy-lyrics-pharrell-williams.html

Happy is defined as "feeling pleasure and enjoyment because of your life, situation, etc.; showing or causing feelings of pleasure and enjoyment; pleased or glad about a particular situation, event, etc." http://www.merriam-webster.com/dictionary/happy

Sometimes, we are so focused in our "pursuit of happiness," we fail to realize that happiness comes from the inside of us.

The NY Times explored this in an article titled *A Formula for Happiness* by Arthur C. Brooks:

"It turns out that choosing to pursue four basic values of faith, family, community and work is the surest path to happiness.

There's nothing new about earned success. It's simply another way of explaining what America's founders meant when they proclaimed in the Declaration of Independence that humans' inalienable rights include life, liberty and the pursuit of happiness.

To pursue the happiness within our reach, we do best to pour ourselves into faith, family, community and meaningful work. To share happiness, we need to fight for free enterprise and strive to make its blessings accessible to all"

http://www.nytimes.com/2013/12/15/opinion/sunday/a-formula-for-happiness.html?pagewanted=1&_r=0

The Bible mentions happiness:

Psalm 144:15 (NKJV): "**Happy** are the people who are in such a state; Happy are the people whose God is the Lord!"

Proverbs 3:13 (NKJV): "**Happy** is the man who finds wisdom, And the man who gains understanding;"

Proverbs 16:20 (NKJV): "He who heeds the word wisely will find good, And whoever trusts in the Lord, **happy** is he."

Wise Quotes include:

*"Folks are usually about as **happy** as they make their minds up to be."* — Abraham Lincoln

*"**Happiness** is when what you think, what you say, and what you do are in harmony."* — Mahatma Gandhi

*"The most important thing is to enjoy your life—to be **happy**—it's all that matters."* — Audrey Hepburn

*"**Happiness** is only real when shared."* — Jon Krakauer, Into the Wild

*"Let no one ever come to you without leaving better and **happier**. Be the living expression of God's kindness: kindness in your face, kindness in your eyes, kindness in your smile."* — Mother Teresa

*"Now and then it's good to pause in our pursuit of **happiness** and just be **happy**."* — Guillaume Apollinaire

Happiness is a Choice…Choose Wisely… ☺

52
"Get Busy Living or Get Busy Dying"

A profound quote from the 1994 movie *Shawshank Redemption* is what wrongly-convicted, 20-year prisoner Andy Dufrense (Tim Robbins) said to his fellow inmate Red (Morgan Freeman): *"Get Busy Living, or Get Busy Dying."*

He went on to tell him in a letter: *"Remember Red, hope is a good thing, maybe the best of things, and no good thing ever dies."*
http://www.imdb.com/title/tt0111161/quotes

Unfortunately, most of us do neither. We are just "busy."

We operate unconsciously…in a fog. Most of our existence consists of looking forward to the future with the goal of "one-day-I'm-gonna." Others are stuck in the past and harboring feelings of "whoa-is-me" and "life is not fair." Some are so mired in their "woulda-shoulda-coulda's" that they become more focused on the past, negativity, regrets and sadness, not realizing how closely they are approaching the end of life.

Basically, all we have is RIGHT NOW. If we don't begin focusing on and enjoying the **here and now**, we will be sadly awaiting our eventual demise.

The Bible warns us of this:

Matthew 6:34 (NKJV): "Therefore do not worry about tomorrow, for tomorrow will worry about its own things. Sufficient for the day is its own trouble."

Quotes to Consider:

"It does not do to dwell on dreams and forget to live." – Albus Dumbledore, Harry Potter and the Sorcerer's Stone

"The trick is to enjoy life. Don't waste away your days, waiting for better ones." – Marjorie Pay Hinckley

"It's only possible to live happily-ever-after on a day-to-day basis." – Margaret Bonnano

"Do not wait until you are ready to DIE to truly learn to LIVE." – Dieter F. Uchtdorf

One of the ways to motivate us to keep moving forward is HOPE. A great acronym for hope is: **H**aving **O**nly **P**ositive **E**xpectations.

Remember: *"Never get so busy making a living that you forget to make a life."* - unknown

So...let's GET BUSY LIVING...

About the Author

Janette McGowen has been writing all of her life, keeping a diary since the age of 6. She made history being only the 2nd female and the 1st African-American Editor-in-Chief of her high school newspaper, which earned state-wide recognition.

She is the third of identical triplets from Lynchburg, TN. Her parents had one son, twins, and finally, triplets. Growing up in a very Christ-centered, close-knit family and in a small town have helped ground her in guiding principles of God, Family and Service.

She earned a Bachelor's Degree in Business Administration from Middle Tennessee State University and an MBA from the University of Phoenix.

Although her professional background has been primarily in the Sales and Marketing sectors, her writing ability has consistently risen to the top. She has written proposals, inquiries, press releases, marketing material and proposals. She was also awarded an "Honorable Mention" for an Inspirational submission in the 80th Annual Writer's Digest Writing Competition.

When McGowen isn't writing, she is nurturing her personal Greeting Card Ministry due to her passionate obsession and desire of staying connected, encouraging and appreciating others. She also loves to read, research, engage in Social Media, serve in her church and study about Holistic Health and Nutrition.

You can contact her at: Janette.McGowen@gmail.com. Her blog can be found at: www.jmacreflections.com

Boothe + Elliot   06-2017

615-957-3867

Made in the USA
Charleston, SC
15 May 2016